Stairway To Hell

The Well-Planned Destruction of Teens

By Rick Jones

The names of the young people discussed in this book (excluding newspaper articles) have been changed to protect their identity.

INTERNATIONAL DISTRIBUTORS

Christ The Way Publications, Inc.
P.O. Box 43120, Eastwood Square
Kitchener, Ont. N5H 6S9, Canada
Tel: (519) 576-2600
Fax: (519) 576-3808

B. McCall Barbour
28 George IV Bridge
Edinburgh, Scotland/UK EH1 1ES
Tel: 0131-225 4816

New Zealand Evangelistic Society
P.O. Box 50096
Porirua, Wellington, New Zealand

Evangelistic Literature Enterprise
P.O. Box 5010
Brendale, Q'ld., Australia 4500
Tel: (07) 3205-7100

BET-EL Multi-Media CC
P/Bag X23227
Gezina 0031, South Africa
Tel: (012) 329-4507
Fax: (012) 329-4510

Chick Gospel Literatur
Postfach 1166
D-51387 Burscheid, Germany
Tel. 02174/63815
Fax: 02174/2799

Chick Publications, Inc.
P.O. Box 3500
Ontario, CA 91761-1100 USA
Tel: (909) 987-0771
Fax: (909) 941-8128

ISBN: 0-937958-30-1

204/F 14th Printing

Published by Chick Publications
P.O. Box 3500, Ontario, CA 91761-1100 USA
Tel: (909) 987-0771 • Fax: (909) 941-8128

Internet: www.chick.com
E-Mail: postmaster@chick.com
Contact author at: rjones@chick.com

Printed in the United States of America

INTRODUCTION

Teenager, this book is for you!

It was written to warn you about the heartbreak and destruction that is sneaking up on you.

Young person, someone is using you, laughing at you behind your back, and playing you for a fool.

The Led Zeppelin song, Stairway To Heaven, is a perfect example of what this book will show you.

The song is a rock classic. It is one of the most famous and often requested songs ever written. Nearly twenty years after it was released, the Los Angeles Times reported that:

> "Young metalmaniacs are so familiar with the 1971 Zeppelin classic 'Stairway To Heaven,' you'd think it was a recent release."[1]

There's one big problem with the song, though.

It is an outright lie!!

It is not a stairway to heaven, it's a stairway to hell.

Millions of young rock fans have heard Robert Plant belt out the following lyrics:

> *"If there's a bustle in your hedgerow*
> *Don't be alarmed now.*
> *It's just a spring clean for the May-*
>   *Queen.*
> *Yes there are two paths you can go by.*
> *But in the long run*
> *There's still time to change the road*
>   *you're on."*

But the real message is heard when that part of the song is played backwards. Here are the devilish lyrics Led Zeppelin has been sneaking into your brain all these years.

As you read this backwards message, remember the song is called, Stairway To **HEAVEN!**

> *"I sing because I live with Satan.*
> *The Lord turns me off.*
> *There's no escaping it.*
> *No other made a path.*
> *Here's to my sweet Satan.*
> *Who's power is Satan.*
> *He will give you 666.*
> *I live for Satan."*

Though it is well disguised, this song is an actual hymn to Satan.

Zeppelin members were servants of Satan. Lead guitarist Jimmy Page owned an occult bookstore in Kensington, England. He also owned and lived in a castle that was once the home of one of the most evil men of the 19th Century, Aleister Crowley, the self-proclaimed Beast 666.[2]

Who **REALLY** wrote this song? Listen to what Robert Plant had to say about how the lyrics came about:

> "I was just sitting there with Page in front of a fire at Headley Grange. Pagey had written the chords and played them for me. I was holding a piece of paper and pencil and for some reason, I was in a very bad mood. Then all of a sudden my hand was writing out the words: 'There's a lady who's sure, that all that glitters is gold, and she's buying a stairway to heaven.' I just sat there and looked at the words and then I almost leaped out of my seat . . . "[3]

Very few people know the true meaning of "Stairway To Heaven." Most look at it as just a classic rock song. But when played backwards, Satan's dark hidden secret comes flying into the bright sunlight.

Millions are deceived by this song. They don't know that every time they play it, two things are happening:

> 1. They are listening to servants of Satan pledge their allegiance to their master.

2. *Listeners are being programmed to accept Satan as the master and destroyer of their own lives.*

Teenager, Wake Up!

The way Satan deceived you in that song is the same way he is deceiving you in your life. While many of your most enjoyable activities seem innocent on the outside, they are really disguised tools of Satan, tools he's using to set you up for destruction.

Believe it or not, the devil has launched an all-out attack to make sure you burn forever in hell. He will stop at nothing to get you there. Unless you find out who's after you, you have no more chance of survival than a palm tree in a frigid Alaska winter.

A war is being fought, young person . . . a war for your soul. Your enemy, Satan, has your destruction all planned out. As long as he can keep you ignorant, he's got you.

Around the world, teenagers are being wiped out in record numbers. They are dying by suicides, drug overdoses, car wrecks, murders, etc. And their deaths are not accidents. They are well planned by Satan.

Will You Be Next?

With those teens safely engulfed in the eternal flames of hell, Satan has now turned his attention towards you. Will you be the next victim?

The Bible warns you to:

"Be sober, be vigilant (watch); because your adversary the devil, as a roaring lion, walketh about, seeking whom he may devour (swallow up):" I Peter 5:8

Ellie never thought she would be one of Satan's victims. She had fine parents, a good home and a bright future. Somewhere along the line, though, she was deceived into living on the stairway to hell.

She did everything she wanted. She tried it all. "I'm running my own life", she excitedly told her friends. Little did she know she had blindly stumbled into Satan's deadly trap.

Though Ellie thought she knew what she was doing, her life turned sour. It always does when you let Satan throw his deadly black cape over your eyes.

Her life fell apart and lost all meaning. Darkness poured into her life. Misery was all she ever felt. But the nightmare was yet to begin.

At the age of 17, it finally happened.

One afternoon she hurried home from school, raced into the house and quickly climbed the stairs to the bathroom before her parents got home.

She threw on some old clothes, dropped her braces in a bowl by the sink, jumped into the bathtub, grabbed a gun, pointed it to her head and pulled the trigger.

Her parents came home to find their young daughter sprawled in a pool of blood in the bathtub . . . dead! They also found a note Ellie had scribbled just before she ended her life. In it she told her parents how sorry she was. She told them she had put on old clothes so she wouldn't ruin any of her good ones.

She suggested they might be able to sell her clothes at a garage sale, and maybe they could return her braces and get their money back. She said she killed herself in the bathtub so she wouldn't get blood all over the carpet and there wouldn't be too much of a mess to clean up.

As you can tell, Ellie was a warm, caring and considerate teenage girl who had everything to live for. Yet for some reason she ended her life. Why? Because she never knew she was in a spiritual war. She lost! She voluntarily died, not knowing she was taking the last fatal step down the dreadful stairway to hell.

She was deceived . . . then destroyed!

This book was written so you won't be the next Ellie. Please read every word of every page very carefully. Your very life and all eternity may well depend on it.

TABLE OF CONTENTS

WHY THIS BOOK?

After working with teenagers at a home for troubled young people for over six years, I learned first-hand that the destruction of teens is not a coincidence.

Their ugly and gruesome deaths are the well planned work of an extremely powerful and unseen enemy.

In those six years, young people with every problem you can imagine passed through my office. From heroin addicts to prostitutes. From those who were physically and sexually abused to those who were locked up in mental institutions. The grizzly list goes on and on.

In all those years, I never met a teen who wanted to end up in the mess they were in. When they eventually hit bottom, they always asked themselves, "How did I end up like this?" And scariest of all, they asked, "Why can't I change now that I see I was deceived?"

It Wasn't Supposed To Be Like This

Connie always wanted to marry a good man and

enjoy a peaceful, happy home. Instead she found herself lying naked and drunk in a pool of vomit on a smelly bathroom floor at a wild party. A drunk man she didn't even know was passed out and lying on top of her.

Within days she was at a clinic being tested for venereal diseases. Obviously, she never dreamed her life would turn out like that.

Day after day, I heard the unbelievably tragic stories. The faces were always different, but the deception, heartbreak and destruction were always the same.

Too many times I listened to young people confess feelings like, "I never thought it would turn out like this," or, "I thought it would be different for me."

Sooner or later they *all* found themselves wondering how they had gotten into such a mess and why they couldn't get out.

As I looked into every desperate and lonely teenage face, I knew there were hundreds and thousands more just like them who were barreling headlong down the same stairway to hell.

And the tragedy was, they didn't have to endure the hell they were living in. The solution was right in front of them.

The purpose of this book, teen, is to show you the solution, along with some cold, hard facts I've learned during my years of working with teens. Hopefully, it will open your eyes and cause you to make some drastic changes in your life before it's too late for you.

Hundreds of teenagers have said to me, "I wish someone had told me these things before I had to go through all this hell." This book will show you where you are headed and what you have to look forward to if you insist on traveling down the stairway to hell.

What you are about to read is the truth, written in an honest, straightforward way. Much of it isn't pleasant reading, but it's still true and you need to hear it.

After six years of seeing deceived teenagers being wiped out on purpose, I must warn you about the deadly snares that have been set for you.

Like a mouse reaching for a tasty piece of cheese, you may be walking into a deadly trap without even knowing it. My desire is to do everything I can to stop you from falling into Satan's deadly trap.

A Satanic Human Sacrifice

Why did three teenage boys you are about to meet beat one of their friends to death with baseball bats? The answer is simple. They were deceived by Satan. They traveled down the stairway to hell and learned the hard way that the devil was planning their destruction all along.

After they murdered their friend, they admitted they

had been tricked by Satan. They confessed that they didn't even know why they had killed him. But it was too late. They had already been sentenced to life in prison with no chance for parole.

The devil has similar plans for you. If you're smart, you won't fall into the same Satanic trap.

Instead, you'll learn from the brutal mistakes of these teens who followed Satan's stairway all the way to committing a satanic human sacrifice.

Teen, don't you wait that long. Keep reading and find out how you can escape from the stairway to hell right now.

Chapter 1

Inside a
Satanic Human Sacrifice

(Reprinted from a two-part article in the Los Angeles Times on October 19 and 20, 1988, entitled Satanists' Trail, Dead Pets to a Human Sacrifice)

"The moon, just out, hung over the Ozarks like a pale opal. Soon families would be saying grace over Sunday dinner; children would be clamoring to turn on the Christmas lights. It was time to go home.

But in the darkening woods, four teenagers lingered, enjoying the rush they always felt when they killed something. A kitten lay crumpled nearby. Sharing some unspoken secret, the boys exchanged furtive glances in the fading light. They were growing edgy. Suddenly, Jim Hardy heard a voice give the command:

"Do it now!"

Jim felt his baseball bat smash into Steven Newberry's face and saw Steve's eyes widen in terror as he cried out, staggered, then turned to run. The others gave chase, sneakers scrabbling madly through the loose gravel and dead leaves. Steve was big and slow. He wheeled around to face his friends as they closed in.

"Why me, you guys?" he begged. "Why me?"

Backing away, Steve tripped. As he fell, he heard a familiar laugh and the answer to his question—a reply bewitchingly soft in the December dusk.

"Because it's fun." Knowing, as they do now,

how brutal and how pointless the murder of Steven Newberry was, the people in this remote speck of southwestern Missouri are filled with grief. There is guilt as well, because it is also clear that his death really was foreseeable.

It took the police, after all, less than a day to follow the whispers and warnings that led to Jim They simply wondered what it would feel like to kill someone. But they also did it out of devotion, for Steven Newberry was dying proof, that winter's eve, of his young friends' faith in Satan.

He was a human sacrifice.

Harder to explain is why no one stepped in to save him.

Jim Hardy

From his cell, (Jim) wrote Pete a letter recently, and admitted that Satan had tricked them.
"I don't even know why we killed Steve", he says now.

Hardy, Pete Roland and Ron Clements, who admitted almost matter-of-factly that they had clubbed Steve to death with baseball bats, tied a 200-pound boulder to his body and dumped him into a well.

They did it, they said, partly out of curiosity:

Aftermath of Guilt

"Everybody is guilty. Everybody is hurt. Everybody feels responsible," Penny Baert said a few days before her son, Pete Roland, began serving time for first-degree murder. "You feel like there's just some small thing you

16

should have done that would have changed everything, and you don't know what it is."

Even now, the people of Jasper County wonder how this Bible Belt hamlet became the moral battleground of a deeply disturbed adolescent subculture . . .

They blame the heavy drug use, the violent music, the forbidden books, the gory movies. And they blame themselves—all the friends, families, teachers, counselors, police, ministers, neighbors and classmates who unwittingly watched three 17-year-olds slip over the edge.

The clues had been mounting for years, telltale signs big and small that stacked up like building blocks. Interviews, police records, public and confidential documents, trial testimony and confessions tell the story.

Many trace the trouble to the day, five years ago, when James Hardy moved his family from Joplin to neighboring Carl Junction, a sleepy suburb whose rambling farms, blue-collar tracts and country club estates brush up against the Kansas border. Hardy was a certified public accountant. He and his wife, Nancy, had three boys and two girls. Their new split-level was surrounded by piney woods and verdant fields. It was a fine place to raise a family.

Start of Rebellion

Jimmy, the second oldest, had been an altar boy and honor student before his grades and behavior took a sudden tumble when he was 11. The nuns at his parish school suggested professional help, and Jim sulked through a few sessions at the Ozark Mental Health Center in Joplin before his exasperated parents gave up.

Nancy and James Hardy had been going through a separation, and assumed the family turmoil had triggered Jim's outbursts. It was the perfect excuse, and no one guessed the truth.

Jim Hardy was a drug

abuser and a sadist. He had been popping pills since the sixth grade. He had been mutilating animals for even longer. These secrets both thrilled and tormented him.

At 13, Jim began getting careless about hiding both his drug habit and his violence. When James Hardy confronted his son about his marijuana use, Jim smashed a baseball bat into his bedroom door with such force that chunks of wood flew into the hall and hit his retreating father.

Outbursts of Temper

The tension between them peaked one day when James Hardy, puttering in the garden, griped about his son's misplacing a tool. Jim stormed cursing into the side yard, where he grabbed a heavy log from the wood pile. He turned to his father.

"I'm going to kill you!" he screamed. He heaved the log against the side of the house and picked up another as his father walked away. This one shattered the sliding glass door.

Remembering this rage brings tears to Jim's eyes now, tears he does not shed when he talks about what he did to Steve Newberry.

Steve was one of the first to befriend Jim when he entered Carl Junction Junior High, but it was Ron Clements who quickly became the closest ally of the weird new kid with the spiked blond hair. Ron's mother was a waitress, and his father was a drifting drug addict who held 30 jobs in four years. Despite their disparate backgrounds, Ron Clements and Jim Hardy forged a blood-brother friendship. Heavy metal music, drug use—and, eventually, Satan—became their common bonds.

Each blames the other for instigating what became an obsession with the occult. It was all talk at first. Then they began pouring over library books on witchcraft and satanism. They repeated chants in vain attempts to summon a demon. They drew pentagrams and other symbols, first on notebook paper, later on buildings. They mimicked the "horned hand" greeting their favorite metal stars flashed at concerts, with pinky and index finger extended and the thumb

was more powerful, and little by little, I fell out of God and started falling into Satan," Jim Hardy recalled. "You can't just dabble. It sucks you in real quick."

In response, Jim thought, Satan gave him more of what he wanted most: Drugs and friends.

"Why me, you guys? Why me?" Ron was laughing. "Because it's fun, Steve!!"

Steve Newberry; the victim

clasped over the other two fingers.

When the bus driver caught Jim preaching satanism to younger children, the school sent a note home, which came back with Nancy Hardy's signature. It didn't change a thing.

"I would kind of just pray to God and Satan at the same time to see who

Ron was praying, too, splaying himself in an upside-down cross on his bed. Believing in Satan could give you so much power, Ron would say, that you could kill someone "with the blink of an eye."

He and Jim agreed that Satan ruled the world.

As sophomores, they grew cockier about their

new-found religion. Each pierced an ear and wore an inverted cross. Jim's, entwined with a serpent, dangled nearly to his shoulder. Ron's was almost hidden by his long, matted hair.

By now, Jim and Ron were mainstays of the "stoner" crowd—the kids who followed the railroad tracks behind Carl Junction High to the woods, where they could sneak a few joints. In class, they were the zombies or the smart alecks. They often spent Saturday morning in detention and Saturday night partying in public parks.

Heavy Metal and Murder

Their favorite bands were the quasi-underground heavy metal groups with names like Megadeth and Slayer. The songs glorified a brand of rebellion that tore at the very soul of church-going communities like Carl Junction. The lyrics tell of seances and Black Masses, of torture and destruction, of Satan—and of sacrifice.

Jim and Ron talked about the macabre constantly . . . Murder intrigued them, and it was almost a competition to see who could come up with the most sadistic fantasy.

"Satan is my lord," Jim would proclaim.

In truth, Ron was starting to get scared.

Late that autumn of his 15th year, Ron came to believe that demons were trying to possess him. He was drifting off to sleep one night when his head began to throb, the pain pounding against his eyes like a jackhammer.

"I felt like there was someone else inside my head . . . but I couldn't understand what they were saying," he told close friends and, later, psychiatrists.

He was dropping out of the satanism thing. Jim was sympathetic. He thought he had been possessed himself half a dozen times.

But Ron's declaration had little effect on his life style. He still liked to party and thrash his head to the music. In detention hall, he filled a school work sheet with satanic pentagrams—five-pointed stars that stand on one point instead of two.

It didn't take Ron long to discover a replacement of sorts for Satan. He had rented the movie "A Clockwork Orange" in the fall of his junior year, then borrowed the Anthony Burgess novel from a friend who never saw it again. The story of teenage sociopaths in a futuristic London excited Ron. He read it over and over, and turned in a book report about getting lost in a novel and becoming a player. Before long, Ron was effecting the Cockney accent and peculiar vocabulary of the novel's anti-hero, a 15-year-old named Alex.

"Alex is my new name and Ron is my forsaken name," Ron declared in the secret journal he was keeping. All entries thereafter were signed "Alex." In a careful, effeminated hand, "Alex" filled the snowy pages with some of the most savage lyrics of the heavy metal movement.

Now Ron claimed he could make out the words of the strange voice inside his head. "Watch out," it urged. "Kill someone." He wondered if it was Alex, and consulted a psychology text for symptoms of insanity.

In April, 1987, Diana and Ron Clements went to the Ozark Mental Health Center for family counseling. Without testing him, the center told the dubious mother it wouldn't be necessary to admit Ron to the drug and alcohol rehabilitation unit, though Ron himself told counselor Randy Grauens in his first session that he wanted to get sober. Grauens doubted Ron's sincerity.

That first meeting, Ron also confided to Grauens . . . that he was consumed by morbid thoughts and fantasies, such as kicking or beating people.

Ozark's initial interview also recorded Ron's fear that he had been demonically possessed, as well as his interest in Satan worship and the occult. This revelation was never explored further.

When Ron went to spend that summer with his father in Arizona, Diana Clements went snooping in her son's bizarre room. Ghastly heavy metal posters were ic descriptions of violence and sexual fantasies were so alarming that she asked a friend at the Carl Junction Police Department what to do. The officer told her Ron needed help.

She took the journal back to the Ozark Center. Randy Grauens didn't find the vulgar entries out

"I felt like there was someone else inside my head . . . but I couldn't understand what they were saying."

Ron Clements

plastered across every spare inch of wall space. Black cloth covered the windows. A stuffed wolf's head hung from the ceiling.

Diaries Dismissed

Diana came across Ron's journal. The graph- of character for a heavy metal fan. The kids called their music "thrash" . . . Ron Clements and Jim Hardy listened for hours at a time and learned the words by heart.

The repulsive songs fed a raw unspeakable hunger that had gnawed at Jim since he was small.

"I was fascinated by death," he recalled. "I always had this obsession with killing things. I don't know, really, what it was. Like, when I started out as a little kid, I couldn't just shoot a bird and watch it die. I had to tear it up. I just thought it was neat. I just wanted to see the death. I was infatuated by the death."

But as Jim grew more popular, death was no longer a secret indulgence. One new friend in particular, Pete Roland, shared his compulsion. Pete was a strapping athlete whose wavy black hair and pale blue eyes earned him first place in the school's Most Photogenic contest, but his milk-fed good looks belied the cruelty within him.

Entertainment at Lunch

Over sack lunches and cafeteria trays, half a dozen or so regulars would listen to Jim talk about torture, apparently never guessing that a few of the animals killed were their own missing pets.

Friends remember sitting in Jim's bedroom and laughing as they watched him drive screws through a Barbie doll's head, then burn the plastic face and wish out loud that it was human.

What would happen if you poured gasoline over an old lady and set her on fire? they speculated.

"People would just trip on it," Jim said. "They thought I was joking, but in my mind, that was exactly what I wanted to do."

"Maybe it was all the drugs and the suggestive music while I was on drugs. Maybe they planted something in my head, but it was also the evil force growing inside me.

"There was something definitely inside me."

Something was changing in Pete, too, and Penny Baert was worried. Her son now emulated Jim's and Ron's disheveled, heavy metal look. He insisted the gory images and satanic symbols on his T-shirts didn't mean a thing.

In his room, Penny

came across crude weapons—broken glass, a stick with nails poking out. The posters on Pete's wall were hideous, like the album covers in his record collection. One showed a singer drinking blood from a human skull.

When she found a satanic bible in Pete's room, Pete quickly explained that it belonged to someone else. After that, it disappeared.

The summer before their senior year, while Ron was away in Arizona, Jim and Pete grew closer. Joined occasionally by other boys in the party crowd—among them Steven Newberry—they tortured animals to death so many times they lost count. Sometimes there were three or four in a day.

Pete and Jim even made up a ditty about their hobby, and each particularly savage episode would merit a new verse. "Sacrifice those babies to Satan . . .," the chorus went. The inspiration had hit Jim and Pete one day after they burned a fluffy little dog alive inside an abandoned dryer they had stuffed with weeds and sprinkled with paint thinner.

"That dog was running around inside and it's the first time I ever heard a dog scream," Jim said. "It sounded just like a human screaming."

"We just started laughing," he added. "That was like a game to us. See how long we could make them live . . . So we just stabbed it a few times and chucked it off into the weeds."

Although he considered himself a devout disciple of Satan at the time, Jim denies the animals were ritualistic sacrifices.

Then, Pete reported that he, too, had heard voices inside his head instructing him to do evil. In exchange for a human sacrifice, Pete believed, Satan would appear and reward him with supernatural powers.

Dr. William Logan . . . hired as an expert witness for Pete's defense, diagnosed Pete as having a psychotic disorder induced by drugs, heavy metal music and Jim Hardy.

Jim came up with a different diagnosis. "It's like, I guess ... something inside me slipped out and grabbed onto Pete."

In fact, Jim's charisma had made him the big man on campus, and he attributed his new-found popularity to Satan "because I was growing in him."

When their senior year began in 1987, the scene at the lunch table was much the same, but human beings began to figure more often in the gruesome "what if" conversations. Many heard (Jim) declare that his life would not be complete until he had killed some-

one. The ultimate goal, Jim boasted, was human sacrifice.

Fears of Insanity

Jim was starting to wonder if he really was crazy. He was asking Satan for more power, and began hearing what he would later describe as a voice inside his head. It told him that he had to prove himself.

One night, Jim became convinced that Satan was wrenching his soul from his body. He was so frightened that he climbed into bed with his dismayed parents. He was 17. "Just watch me during the night while I

"Music boomed from the tape deck. A line from one of the songs would later haunt Pete, the one that went, "dying time is here."

Pete Rowland

sleep," he asked, "and wake me up if it looks like I'm having any trouble."

Although his parents were puzzled, Jim made no secret of "the voice" at school. He told classmates who teased him about his "invisible friend" that it was no figment of his imagination. The friend, unbidden, would appear and make him do things, Jim said.

When one girl asked Jim if it was true that he sacrificed cats, he said yes, that he liked to taste the blood because it was sweet. What about dogs, she asked. Their blood was just as good. What about humans?

"Haven't gotten to them yet," Jim replied.

Jim now denies he ever drank blood and complains that many classmates gave false statements against him.

Part 2

'Fun' Killers Now Paying Devil's Dues

The "action"- as student body president Jim Hardy now calls the bludgeoning death of Steven Newberry—began to unfold with a casual conversation among seven classmates one September afternoon. Jim and his best friends, Pete Roland and Rom Clements, were there, and the talk, as usual, was about killing. But this time, it wasn't just the twisted fantasies of tough teenagers fixated on drugs, acid rock and violence. This time, it would be self-fulfilling prophecy.

This time, Steve Newberry would die, and with him, the innocence of the Bible Belt town where his killers and a number of his classmates openly dabbled in satanism.

The kids were trying to think of someone to sacrifice. A 14-year-old girl named Angel jokingly nominated Steve, since Jim and his pals were always talking about how much they hated him.

No, Jim decided, they would keep Steve around for his drugs.

If Jim Hardy was the stoners' hero, Steve Newberry was the scapegoat. Overweight and careless about his hygiene, Steve was what the kids called a wannabe. And what he wanted to be was a part of Jim Hardy's crowd.

Marlys Newberry, twice divorced, with four teenagers, was well aware that her eldest child, Steven, was smoking pot, but apparently didn't realize that psychedelic drugs, barbiturates, cocaine and amphetamines were also being used by the stoner crowd Steve so ardently pursued. What really alarmed Marlys was the heavy metal music Steve listened to for hours on end. She would go through his tapes with him and throw away the "thrash," telling her indignant son that it would put ideas in his mind.

When they argued, Steve would sometimes stalk out and spend the night with a friend.

"I think you better just stay away from them," Marlys warned. Steve had told her all about the Hardy crowd's interest in satanism and Jim's ultimate goal of killing someone, and she could see how Steve would be the perfect candidate.

"Jim's my friend," Steve protested. "He wouldn't do that."

. . . That holiday weekend (Thanksgiving, 1987) marked the third try on Steven Newberry's life in less than a month.

At school that week, the boys discussed their latest failure and rescheduled Steven Newberry's murder for that Sunday.

"Every time we failed, I don't know what drove us, but we wanted that experience," said Jim. "We just had to have that experience. I know it had to spring from Satan."

On Friday night, the stoners got rowdy at a party. Jim, drunk on whiskey, kept telling Ron what a good friend he was.

"I can't wait till Sunday," he said.

Weekend of the Killing

Sunday dawned sunny and clear. It was Dec. 6.

The Newberry's went to church and came home for

an early supper. Marlys had roasted a turkey. She went back to church that afternoon to rehearse her second-grade Sunday school class for the Christmas pageant.

Jim called Steve . . . and said they were going out to kill something, if Steve wanted to come along.

At the Newberry house, Jim went up to the door while Ron and Pete listened to heavy metal in the car. Marlys didn't like the idea of Steven going out with those boys, and told him he knew exactly why. Marlys, too tired to argue, told him he was 19 and could make his own decisions.

Steve crawled into the back of Pete's maroon Datsun. Four baseball bats lay on the floor and Ron held up his for Steve to see. "Ultraviolence was written on it . . ." Music boomed from the tap deck.

> *"You can't just dabble (in satanism). It sucks you in real quick."*
> Jim Hardy

A line from one of the songs would later haunt Pete, the one that went, "dying time is here."

They parked on the soft shoulder of the road and hiked the half-mile through the brush and bramble to the Well of Hell. Pete had brought a roll of twine, and they tied the bagged kitten from a tree, taking turns hitting it like a pinata. When it was dead, they took it down and tossed it aside.

Jim tells the rest of the story from the federal penitentiary:

Steve spoke first, saying he wished they had "something bigger to kill."

In that instant, Jim heard the voice inside his head, the one that always told him to prove himself.

"Do it now!"

Jim felt the bat strike Steve's face.

As they chased him down, Steve stumbled

28

through the dark, asking his pursuers the same thing over and over. "Why me, you guys? Why me?" Ron was laughing. "Because it's fun, Steve," he said.

"The way Clements said it," Jim recalled, "it was real soothing, like you'd talk to a little kid. 'Because it's fun, Steve.' I think that just freaked Steve out, because he kinda stopped and turned around, like, maybe they're not going to kill me after all."

Pete would later confess that they hit Steve about 70 times, fracturing his skull so severely that one of the bats broke and someone had to grab the one Steve had dropped to continue.

When the frenzy was over. Steve was still moaning. Jim Hardy took a bloody bat and nudged him in the shoulder.

"Sacrifice to Satan," he said.

Sounds of Dying

The boys took turns dragging the body back to the well. Ron noticed Steve's fingers scraping the dirt, as if escape were still possible. The sounds of death were getting on Ron's nerves. "Shut up, Steve!" he barked, and kicked him in the face.

Back at the car, Ron, fearing Satan might possess him again, issued a cool disclaimer:

"Jim, I didn't do this as a sacrifice to Satan," he said. "I did it for my own personal gratification."

Jim didn't care. He was sure he had appeased the voice inside his head. This, he figured, was "the ultimate proof."

Returning to the Hardy house, Ron rinsed the blood from his face and hands in the bathroom sink. Pete and Jim didn't notice any on themselves, nor did Jim's parents. They scolded Jim for being late. They had saved him some spaghetti for dinner.

Lance Owens had gone to Pete's that (Monday) morning for a ride to school, and Pete had told him all about the murder. In art class, Jim also told

Lance, crowing, "We did it! We did it!" After art Ron asked Lance to be his new locker partner. Steve's things were still inside.

Steve's younger sister, 14-year-old Christina, called her mother from school that afternoon with disturbing news. Three friends of hers had overheard Jim and Pete laughing in the hall. They were saying something about stabbing a fat person to death.

Carl Junction, home to nearly 4,000 mostly God-fearing people, took the tragedy hard. Word that the slaying was somehow linked to satanism whipped through town like a spring storm.

Bizarre Things Remembered

Dozens of adults around Jasper County began telling authorities about bizarre occurrences they hadn't considered reporting until now: naked people chanting in the woods, dog heads hanging from cave entrances, kids in robes killing animals in an old schoolhouse, a slaughtered rabbit on a front porch with "Die" written in blood, piles of skinned dogs with their hearts cut out, satanic graffiti everywhere.

A close friend of Jim Hardy's summed up the feelings of many stoners who, like him, had enjoyed the morbid fantasies and animal tortures. He still does. Unable to fully comprehend or control these urges, he is terrified.

"Whatever it is inside of him that made him do that," he says, "we all have inside us."

By summer, the drama was over. Jim Hardy had accepted the prosecutor's deal and would plead guilty in exchange for life without parole. Clements and Roland turned the offer down, deciding to risk the death penalty by standing trial. Their insanity pleas were brushed aside by juries that handed down verdicts of life without parole.

From his cell, (Jim) wrote Pete a letter recently, and admitted that

Satan had tricked them.

"I don't even know why we killed Steve," he says now. "It was like any other animal we killed."

Jim never did feel the surge of power he thought Satan had promised him in exchange for the ultimate proof. Not long ago, the voice came back, the one that told him to do it now.

Hears Satan's Whisper

Softly he repeats the words he insists Satan whispered inside his troubled young mind:

"Just open the door once and I promise I'll never let you go."

Marlys Newberry never heard her son's voice after that Monday morning when she distinctly heard him whimper, "Mom."

She remembers going to Sears not long after Steven died. She wanted to buy detergent. With a houseful of teenagers, she always got the giant 48-pound box.

"I could scarcely pick up that box of detergent. And by the time I got to the car, tears were running down my face, because Steven had always carried it for me. 'Mom, it's too heavy for you, let me.' I had never lifted that box before, myself.

"I didn't know how heavy it was."

> *"Softly, (Jim) repeats the words he insists Satan whispered inside his young mind:*
> *"Just open the door once and I promise I'll never let you go."*

31

By the millions, teens around the world are being deceived into traveling down Satan's stairway to hell.

This newspaper article is just one example. These young people followed the devil's carefully-laid steps, one by one, straight downhill to destruction.

In the following pages, we will look at each of the steps they took. Remember, this is Satan's top secret plan for destroying teens. He does not want you to read this book.

Teen, you are on a very real stairway to hell. The devil hates you and wants you to burn in hell. That's all he cares about.

Hopefully, after reading this book, you won't be the next Jim, Ron or Pete. Or even worse, the next Steve.

Chapter 2

The Top Secret Plan

*"**O**h, God! No! No! No!*

"This can't be happening to me! Total blackness! Terrifying screams!

"God! Please get me out of here! I'm on fire!

"The flames are sizzling me! The smoke is choking me! The stench of burning flesh is turning my stomach!

"I can't stand this pain. Somebody get me out of here!"

This is a gruesome description of one more teenager who just took the last fatal step down the eternally damning stairway to hell.

This poor sap discovered a little too late that he had been deceived by someone who hated him and had devised a plan to make him suffer forever.

Now, his agonizing screams for mercy are useless. It's too late! He will spend the rest of eternity, for ever and ever, trapped and burning in this very real lake of fire, with no way to escape . . . ever! But he will keep screaming anyway:

> "Oh, God, I'm sorry. I beg you to get me out of this fire!
>
> I was so stupid! Why didn't I see it? What a fool I was!"

If this condemned teen could deliver one message to you from this place of torment, he would scream out:

> "Teenager, don't come here! Don't get fooled like I did! Wake up! Get off the stairway to hell before it's too late!"

How did this young person end up in the most wicked place of torture in the entire universe? Very simply, he followed a carefully laid plan. He walked, step by step, straight down the devil's stairway to hell, a stairway that descends right into the never-dying flames of hell.

Tragically, he is not the only teenager who has reached this flaming prison. Millions of others have retraced his bloodstained steps to this dark, fiery pit.

Today, parents around the world are crying out: "What's happening to our kids? Why are they dying?"

Let's find out right now.

Your Unseen Enemy

Teenagers today are being chewed up and spit out by a powerful enemy they don't even know they have. They don't stand a chance against him and his army.

Like sheep headed for the slaughter, millions of gullible teens have proudly marched down his stairway, deceived into thinking they know what they are doing.

The group "Megadeth" gives teens this severe warning. Their song, "Good Mourning, Black Friday" says:

> *"Killer, intruder, homicidal man*
> *If you see me coming, run as fast as you*
> * can*
> *A blood-thirsty demon who's stalking the*
> * street*
> *I hack up my victim's like pieces of*
> * meat."*

If only teens knew what Satan had in store for them before it was too late.

While working with troubled teens, I lived with the tragedy of destroyed teenage lives day and night. The names were always different, but their path to destruction was always the same.

After doing hundreds of intake interviews and listening to thousands of depressing life stories, it became obvious that these young lives were not being ruined by accident. Their stories were almost always identical because they all had the same enemy (Satan), and he always uses the same top secret plan.

As long as the devil can keep teenagers from finding out that behind the scenes, he is plotting their destruction, they are sitting ducks, waiting to be blown into oblivion.

Before you scoff, teen, you better think twice, because that's the exact response Satan wants you to have. If he can stop you from believing what you are about to read, he's already got you. He'll have no trouble getting you to follow the teen at the beginning of this chapter into the scorching flames of hell.

The Bible gives you fair warning that you are engaged in spiritual warfare:

> *"For we wrestle not against flesh and blood, but against principalities, against powers, against the rulers of the darkness of this world, against spiritual wickedness in high places."* *Ephesians 6:12*

Teen, Satan has a carefully laid plan for **your** eternal destruction. He's counting on you being stupid enough not to know what he's up to.

I hope you'll be smarter than to let him suck you into hell. Your choice is simple. Reject the devil's lies and live, or swallow them . . . and burn forever.

You can say, "I don't believe it," slam this book shut and forget it. But someday you'll die and stand before God. Then you will see, like the teen at the beginning of this chapter, that you were tricked. Then you'll know the Bible was right when it said:

> *"The wicked shall be turned into hell."*
> Psalm 9:17

> *"Fear him, (God) which after he hath killed hath power to cast into hell; yea, I say unto you, Fear him."* Luke 12:5

> *"And death and hell were cast into the lake of fire. And whosoever was not found written in the book of life was cast into the lake of fire."* Revelation 20:14,15

Teenager, my desire is that you will read this book, believe what the Bible says, and escape from the alluring stairway that's taking you to the most horrid place ever made . . . the burning flames of hell.

There's only one reason anyone would willingly stay on the stairway to hell . . . they've been tricked. Let's see how Satan gets teens like you to hop on that stairway . . . and then stay there.

You can be sure the devil will do everything he can to stop you from reading about his top secret plan for killing teens.

Don't let him stop you!

Chapter 3

Why Can't Parents & Teens Get Along?

"Get off my case!"

"You just don't understand me!"

"Why don't you leave me alone!"

The sounds of a parent-teenage war. There's yelling, screaming, doors slamming, tempers flaring, faces beet-red, you know the symptoms.

Why can't teens and their parents get along?

Two Groups

That's a tough question because there are two different groups of parents. First are the parents who are totally unfit to raise children. Sad to say, millions of teens grow up in homes like this.

Most people have no idea the living hell thousands of youngsters are enduring. Nobody knows better than kids how sick this world is. They are the ones who **always** end up paying the price.

For millions of teens, the pain and suffering starts young. Look at just a few of the epidemic parent-related problems teens are facing today:

* *Being forced into prostitution by their parents for the money.*

* *Incest. No one knows how many millions of children are scarred for life through sexual abuse by their own parents.*

* *Children introduced to homosexuality and lesbianism by their parents.*

* *Children who get hooked on drugs through their parents.*

* *Kids who are physically beaten by parents.*

* *"Throwaways." Children tossed out on the streets to fend for themselves by uncaring parents.*

* *Untold thousands of youngsters are sold into Satan worship by depraved parents.*

Teen, if you are suffering today, you are **not** alone. Millions of teens are in the same boat. If you know your parents couldn't care less about you, this chapter is not for you. Keep reading, though, because I'll walk down your street a little later.

If Your Parents Really Do Care

This chapter is for teens with parents who do care. They love their kids and want the best for them. Their hearts break when they see them being led astray.

Tragically, Satan is a master at making teens think their parents don't care about them when they really do. So teen, before you toss your parents into the "couldn't care less about me" category, read this.

Though I've heard thousands of teens try to explain why they couldn't get along with their parents, in six years, not one ever hit the nail on the head.

I've listened to excuses like:

* *"My parents just don't understand me."*
* *"I've got to do my own thing."*
* *"My parents haven't earned my respect, so I don't have to do what they say."*

I've heard every reason in the book for the parent-teenage war . . . every one, that is, but the real one.

The Real Reason

Parents and teens can't get along because quietly, behind the scenes, the evil one is doing everything he can to break up homes and destroy parent - teenage relationships.

Teen, if Satan can wreck your relationship with your parents, he just got you to take that all-important first step onto the stairway to hell.

Now you're on your way down. Look out, it gets rough from here. It may not seem that bad now, but just wait till you see where the devil is leading you.

When your parents see you speeding down the on-ramp to the stairway to hell, they will do everything they can to warn you.

To stop you from listening to those warnings, Satan convinces you that your parents "just don't understand you" or "don't care about you."

Once he's gotten you to believe that lie, he can keep you on his deadly path. You will ignore your parents' warnings and will stumble straight down, convinced you are doing the right thing. In reality, you are walking Satan's well-worn stairway to destruction.

Judy, a high school sophomore, wrote the lyrics to a heavy metal song in her journal. It was her last entry. She killed herself in a suicide pact with her boyfriend. She said she worshiped the devil, but never bothered to talk to her parents because they "wouldn't understand."

Not Your Thoughts

Cutting off communication is the first step on Satan's stairway. Your death and torture in hell is the last one. Remember, teen, when thoughts rush into your mind like, "My parents don't care about me" or "they don't want me to have any fun," those are **not** your thoughts. Satan put those thoughts in your mind to trick you into taking the first step on his stairway.

If he can get you to take that first step, he can lead you down to the last one.

Do you have a problem obeying your parents, teen? Have you ever felt, "they just don't understand me?" Do you rebel against everything they say? If so, it's not an accident. It's the result of hard work by your unseen enemy.

What a devilishly clever plan! No one can convince you to get off the stairway to hell because in your mind you know exactly what you are doing. You're convinced that the problem is "nobody understands me." You don't have a problem; everybody else does.

I've seen the devil use that dirty tactic more times than I could count. Somehow, I know he gets a hearty chuckle every time it works.

While you cling to catch-phrases like, "I've got to do my own thing," you are really doing Satan's thing, and diving head-first down his stairway.

Teen, you took your first dreaded step onto the devil's stairway when you let Satan ruin your relationship with your parents. Now you're headed for big trouble.

Must Get You To Disobey God

There's someone else the devil must get you to reject if he is to destroy you. This person loves you and wants to protect you from Satan. His name is God. For your protection from Satan's snares, God says you should:

" . . . *obey your parents in the Lord: for*

this is right . . . That it may be well with thee, and thou mayest live long on the earth."   Ephesians 6:1,3

"My son, hear the instruction of thy father, and forsake not the law of thy mother:"   Proverbs 1:8

To persuade you to reject God's warnings and open you up for destruction, the devil has another convincing lie. He plants the thought in your mind, "Don't listen to God, He doesn't want you to have any fun."

Like a hungry fish lunging for fresh bait, gullible teens have swallowed that lie, hook, line and sinker.

Teenager! Wake up!!

You are being lied to!!

You are being set up for the kill!!

You may think you're doing "your thing," but you're really doing "Satan's thing," just like he wants you to. You are on the stairway to hell! And the steps get continually steeper from here.

It's no coincidence that millions of teens can't get along with their parents. It's step number one of Satan's master plan to get you on the deception-filled stairway to hell.

Young person, if your relationship with your parents

is in bad shape, it's because Satan is at work. Please realize who's manipulating you and stop your downward spiral right now. Get to your parents and make things right with them.

If you don't want to be destroyed, don't let your enemy win a victory by getting you on his stairway.

Even Alice Cooper tried to tell you the result of rebelling against your parents. Look what he says in the song, "Go To Hell," from his album, "Alice Cooper Goes To Hell."

> " . . . *For gambling and drinking alcohol constantly*
> **For making us doubt our parent's authority**
> *For choosing to be a living obscenity*
> **You can go to Hell . . .** "

Alice, you are right. If only teens would listen.

Chapter 4

Nobody's Gonna Tell
<u>Me</u>
What To Do!

Heavy metal rockers, Twisted Sister, have a song and video titled *We Ain't Gonna Take It*. In the video, a teenage boy drags his father through their home by his hair and heaves him out a second story window.

The song's theme can be summed up in one word:

Rebellion!

In fact, the theme of not only that song, but the whole group and all other rock groups is the same: rebellion.

* *Rebellion against parents.*
* *Rebellion against the law.*
* *Rebellion against school.*
* *Rebellion against society.*

For the last 25 years, this rebellion philosophy has been shoved at teenagers like food down a crying baby's throat.

A teen who submits to any kind of authority today is treated like a weirdo. It just isn't "cool" (or whatever term you like) to be in obedience to others.

Teens world-wide have uttered the "intellectual" reasons for why they act this way:

* *"I'm old enough to make my own decisions!"*
* *"I've got to do what I feel is right."*
* *"You just wouldn't understand."*

So many times I've gazed into the eyes of a rebellious teen and thought, "You poor teen. You think you've got it together but you're so deceived. Satan is laughing at you and you don't have any idea what's going on. You're doing what your spiritual master (Satan) wants so he can destroy you . . . and you have no idea what's happening."

How sad! How tragic!

You see, teenager, the outbreak of blatant rebellion among teens today is not an accident. It's planned! It's a vital part of Satan's plan for your destruction.

Whether you realize it or not, when you rebel against authority, you are disobeying the instructions God gave to protect you from your enemy and you are opening yourself up for demonic destruction. Listen to what God says about rebellion:

> *"For rebellion is as the sin of witchcraft..."*
> *I Samuel 15:23*

49

In God's eyes, to rebel against His commands is just as bad as being into Satan worship. Millions of teens have thought, "I'll never get involved in Satan worship." Yet they rebel against parents, teachers, etc., not knowing their rebellion is just as dangerous.

> *"Woe to the rebellious children, saith the Lord, that take counsel, but not of me."*
> *Isaiah 30:1*

> *"Such as sit in darkness and in the shadow of death, being bound in affliction and iron; Because they rebelled against the words of God . . ."*
> *Psalm 107:10-11*

Because God wants to protect you from the devil, He gives you some very important instruction:

> *"Obey them that have the rule over you, and submit yourselves..."Hebrews 13:17*

> *"Likewise, ye younger, submit yourselves unto the elder."* *I Peter 5:5*

God's commands of obedience are for your protection, not to stop you from having fun. They were written so you could enjoy real fun.

A dad called one day, begging us to help his teenage daughter. When the girl found out about the call, she ran away from home. She wasn't going to let her father "ruin" her fun. She wanted to do her own thing.

For months the dad heard nothing from his daughter. One day he called us again. His teenage daughter had been found . . . ice cold and dead in a morgue in a distant state.

No wonder Satan has put such an emphasis on rebellion. It's another key to your destruction. It's one of the widest steps on the stairway to hell. If the devil can't get you to rebel, he can't kill you.

Turn on MTV for an hour. What's the message? Rebellion against authority, against society, against parents, against almost everything, except rock music.

Television pushes rebellion. Movies push rebellion. No matter where you turn, the same Satanic message is being pounded into young brains: "Don't let **anyone** tell you what to do! You have your rights! It's your life!"

Tim swallowed that lie and adopted the "it's my life" philosophy when he was about nine. The older he got, the more rebellious he became. He did whatever he wanted.

For a while he thought he had it made . . . total freedom. But while he was doing "his" thing (really, he was a pawn doing Satan's thing), his life was falling apart around him.

His rebellion got him tossed out of both his home and every school in his area. He hated a boss telling him what to do, so he couldn't hold a job. Getting cold and hungry, he turned to the only way of making money he could find, homosexual prostitution.

His dreams turned to nightmares. He lived in slimy, rat-infested run down holes. A never-ending parade of lust-filled perverts poured through his room, each vile experience leaving him feeling sicker and dirtier than the one before.

The last time I heard from him, he was still walking the streets of a major city as a homosexual prostitute, dressed as a female. He said he was afraid he had AIDS and wished he could die. His life was ruined.

He rebelled and did what he wanted. But it didn't turn out like he thought it would. **It never does when you listen to the devil's lies!!**

I know "submission to authority" is not a popular message these days. But I'd rather tell you the truth and warn you where you're headed than to say nothing and see you follow Tim's path. Before you say, "I'd never do that," guess what; that's what Tim said.

I recently dealt with a very rebellious young man. He flatly stated, "I can't stand anybody telling me what to do." Because of his rebellious spirit, he was recruited into the occult. Satanists love rebellious teens.

He soon saw what Satanism was all about (from the inside) and got scared to death. He literally ran for his life. He fled the state with just the clothes on his back. Rebellion had taken its toll. It *always* does.

Teenager, I've seen it too many times to count. Rebellion *always* leads to ruin! Every single time. God promised it would . . . and He's right.

If you have a rebellious spirit, Satan is in control of your life. You may be proud of your independent, rebellious nature now, but as you slide farther down Satan's slippery stairway, you will curse the day you ever gave the devil that much control of your life.

Rebellious teen, you may think you are impressing your friends, but you are really a great big sap, playing right into the devil's hands.

Boy, are you in for a big surprise.

Chapter 5

Peer Pressure:
The Invisible Glue

"My life really took a nose dive when I started hanging around with the wrong crowd."

One thing you can count on teen, Satan will use your "friends" to get and keep you on the stairway to hell. There's no debating it, what your friends are today, you will be tomorrow.

* Hang with the drug crowd and you will be taking drugs before you know it.

* Become friends with thieves and you will be stealing before you can say, "shoplifting."

It is a sad fact that most teenagers are hopeless followers, searching frantically for someone to lead them. Satan is more than willing to provide the leadership they are looking for.

Your enemy knows that if he's going to keep you riding down the stairway to hell, he'll have to use some of your peers who have already swallowed his lies to suck you down too. Enter the invisible glue that holds Satan's master plan all together . . .

. . . peer pressure!

Everyone wants to be liked and popular. No one likes being laughed at, especially during junior and senior high years. Everybody wants to be accepted and part of the "in" crowd. Nobody wants to be an outsider. (Remember Steve Newberry in chapter one?)

How well your enemy knows this and uses it to his advantage. Sometimes it seems teenagers will do **anything** to belong. Teens like Steve have been literally beaten to death in an effort to belong.

How funny it is to watch a young person inhale their first cigarette. They choke, turn blue, nearly throw up and get sick to their stomach. But to impress their friends, they keep at it.

I remember a teen's first "drinking" experience. He and several friends stood shivering outside a car on a deserted road in sub-zero temperatures. As he took his first swig of ice cold beer, he wanted to spit it out. It tasted terrible. He was already freezing, and the last thing he wanted was a cold beer.

Then the thought popped into his mind, "What will my friends think?" So he downed that beer and several more that were shoved at him. He later confided that it was the most miserable night of his life.

The next day he bragged to all his friends about what a great time he and his buddies had the night before. Everyone was jealous. If only they knew the truth.

Today, while millions of teens are striving to be part of the "in" crowd, most never realize that the crowd they long to be a part of is the crowd that is tumbling out of control down the stairway to hell.

When I was in high school, if you made the "A" honor roll (a problem I never had), you were looked down upon and sneered at by many. But if you got arrested or thrown out of a few classes, you were a school hero. It should be the other way around, but who cares if it means being a part of the "in" crowd.

As you've probably figured out by now, peer pressure is not an accident either; it is another of your enemy's powerful tools. When you give in to peer pressure, you've not only played into the devil's hand, you've also kicked aside sincere warnings from God about the consequences.

Throughout the Bible, God tells you to steer clear of those who do wrong because He knows the tremendous power of peer pressure. And whether you're "in" or "out," "cool" or a weirdo, your destruction will be just as painful and just as real.

Look what God tells you to do for your protection:

> *"My son, if sinners entice thee, consent thou not . . . walk not thou in the way with*

them; refrain thy foot from their path: For their feet run to evil, and make haste to shed blood."   *Proverbs 1:10,15-16*

"Enter not into the path of the wicked, and go not in the way of evil men. Avoid it, pass not by it, turn from it, and pass away."   *Proverbs 4:14-15*

"Blessed is the man that walketh not in the counsel of the ungodly, nor standeth in the way of sinners, nor sitteth in the seat of the scornful . . . For the Lord knoweth the way of the righteous: but the way of the ungodly shall perish."
    Psalm 1:1,6

Found Out A Little Too Late

Denise wanted to be accepted. Her parents were wealthy and she had everything except a rich and handsome boyfriend. She couldn't adequately impress her friends without one.

When a potential "Mr. Wonderful" came along, she couldn't bear the thought of letting him get away. "Anything to keep him," she thought.

Before she knew it, she was pregnant. Things were not going the way she had planned. They never do when you buy Satan's goods. Her mom pressured her to have an abortion. Since she didn't want to be "tied down" with a baby and give up her "fun," she did.

When she awoke after the abortion, she began weeping uncontrollably. All at once it hit her like an exploding atomic bomb. She had taken the devil's bait. She realized she had been gravely deceived and knew she had murdered a precious and innocent little life, her own baby.

She found out what Satan was up to, but it was a few minutes too late. Her little baby was already in a garbage bag and on its way to the dumpster. The devil was undoubtedly laughing happily that he had snuffed out another young life.

I Must Impress My Friends

Tom had a problem. He wanted to have friends. He watched some kids at school who were really "cool." They seemed to be having a lot of fun and everybody wanted to be part of their group.

Tom heard that to be accepted by that group, you had to smoke, so he started smoking. Then he heard you had to drink, so he did that too. Next he learned that to be really "cool," you had to run away from home. He did that too.

Then, to really impress them, he began smoking pot. The "cool" kids responded and soon he was one of the "cool" ones too. He was "Mister Popular."

Now that he had a reputation, he had to keep it. More powerful drugs, dealing drugs, and crime followed. Everybody was very impressed. He was extra cool.

Stairway To Hell

Little did Tom or any of his friends realize that Satan was using peer pressure to destroy another young life. When Tom died of a drug overdose, the devil had the last laugh. Tom wasn't cool. He was a fool. Peer pressure had killed another one.

Teenager, if Satan has gotten you hanging with the wrong crowd today, he will use peer pressure tomorrow to drag you down his stairway to hell.

I've dealt with hundreds of teens who thought they would be the first to play with fire and not get burned. They *all* got sizzled. There are *no* exceptions.

When you let peer pressure cause you to do something you shouldn't do, you are not saying yes to your friends, you are saying yes to Satan. You are also taking another giant step down the ever-darkening stairway to hell.

You may laugh about it now, but keep reading. You won't be laughing soon. Your enemy, the devil, will have the last laugh as he sees your squirming body being tossed into the eternally burning lake of fire.

Chapter 6

Hey, This Is Fun!

61

The first night Mary got high with her friends, it was great. She laughed harder than she had in years. She told corny jokes and forgot all her problems.

She felt totally free. It was one of the most enjoyable nights of her life.

As she sat cross-legged on the floor in that dimly lit smoke-filled living room, her parents' stern warnings about the dangers of drugs flashed through her mind. "How wrong they are," she chuckled to herself. "If only they knew . . . this is really fun."

The next morning she was still glowing. She could hardly wait 'til Friday night when she could do it again. "At last," she sighed, "I've found something that makes me really happy."

Teenager, Mary just took another giant leap down the stairway to hell. Tragically, she had no idea that she was being set up.

You see, whenever Satan sets the trap for you, he will

always make it look like fun in the beginning. To a hungry rat, that first bite of cheese tastes delicious, until the lightning-fast spring snaps over his head and a piece of cold steel crushes his neck.

The same is true of your enemy, Satan. No matter which of his deceptive tactics he uses on you, it will always be fun in the beginning.

I once asked a former heroin addict how he ever got himself to drive a needle into his arm and risk his entire life. He told me it wasn't like that when he started. In the beginning it was fun. He smoked pot and had a great time. The problem was that the fun soon ended and misery took its place.

Once he was addicted, he'd do **anything** to get high. It wasn't for fun anymore. Now it was survival.

It Used To Be Fun

An ex-prostitute learned the same lesson. Continual running away led her into the nightmare of prostitution. But the first time she ran away it was great. She fled to a girlfriend's house where she played records, ate, giggled, stayed up late and did whatever she wanted.

That night, Satan planted a deadly lie in her impressionable mind. She thought to herself:

> *"Running away is fun. My parents were wrong, it's not dangerous. They just*

don't want me to have any fun."

Eventually she was forced into prostitution. Her life was total misery! She was beaten regularly by her pimp and shoved out to the cold streets every night in the skid row sections of town to "work."

After enduring sex with untold numbers of creeps each night, she was forced to give her pimp every penny she had made when she returned "home."

Things sure had changed from that first night at her girlfriend's house. They always do when you buy the devil's lies.

I don't imagine the teenager who blew his brains out while listening to an Ozzy Osbourne album with his head phones on ever dreamed it would end like that the day he listened to his first rock music album.

The manager of a B. Dalton Bookstore said teens come in her store and ask for the satanic bible a lot. Why? She said, "I think it's more fad than serious interest . . . "[1] In other words, it looks like fun.

Thousands of teens are being engulfed in the horrors of Satanism because it looks like it will be fun. You may think it's just a fad when you start, but that will quickly change. Once Satan sinks his hook in your jaw, reels you in and slams you on the floor of his boat, you'll see what satanism is really like.

If only young people had the wisdom to look past the

first few feet and soo themselves down the road participating in their first satanic human sacrifice.

Regardless of which of his snares Satan sets for you, you can be sure of one thing . . . it will be fun in the beginning. But just as surely, your fun will be transformed into a nightmare before your very eyes. Nothing you can do will change that fact.

You say, "I get high," or "I rebel against my parents, and I'm doing O.K." Just hang on, teenager, your day is coming.

Sooner or later, that steel trap will crush your head and before you know what hit you . . . waap . . . you will have just become Satan's latest victim.

The first step is fun, but the last one will leave you screaming in agony for ever.

Chapter 7

"I Got Ya"

Satan rockers AC/DC sing a song called, Hell's Bells. The lyrics go like this:

"Satan's gonna get you
Gonna drag you to Hell
No one's puttin up a fight
You get into evil
You're a friend of mine . . .
I'm gonna take you to Hell
Gonna get ya
Satan got ya
Hell's Bells . . . "

While I worked with troubled young people, I saw many patterns, but one in particular sent cold shivers up and down my spine.

Teenagers who violated God's commands and participated in Satanic activities did so at first because they wanted to. The only reason they didn't stop was because they didn't want to stop.

But those who continued to rebel against God eventually reached a point where they could not stop what they were doing, even though they desperately wanted to.

Bob is a perfect example. He was sexually molested as a young child. By the age of 9 he was obsessed with pornography. It was "fun" at first, but the longer he looked at it, the greater the hold it got on him.

As his lust grew, he began sexually abusing other children. When he finally got caught, he was in shock. His parents were humiliated and his father was fired from his job because of it.

Bob realized how sick and perverted it was, but he couldn't stop, though he wanted to more than anything else in the world. No matter how hard he tried, it kept happening.

He Couldn't Stop Himself

One day, while walking with an 8-year-old girl in the woods, he said something strange came over him. He honestly did not want to hurt this child but he couldn't stop himself. Though he tried not to, he sexually molested her.

Afterwards, he was sick. He hated himself so much for what he had done that he wanted to die. In fact, he tried to commit suicide more than once. He hated himself with a passion. He went to doctors, psychiatrists and psychologists, but nobody could help him.

My question was, "Why couldn't he just stop if he didn't want to do it anymore?" It seemed simple enough. All he'd have to say is, "I don't like it and I don't want to do it anymore, so I won't."

But I had asked myself very similar questions hundreds of times before:

> * *Why couldn't teens stop taking drugs when they finally figured out that the drugs were destroying them? Why would a teen risk dying from a drug overdose by sticking a dirty needle in his arm?*

> * *Why couldn't boys leave the homosexual lifestyle when they learned how deviate and miserable it really is? Why couldn't they quit? While he was lying in some cheap backstreet motel with a dirty greaseball on top of him, why couldn't a guy just say, "No more! I quit!"*

One day I got the answer from a lady who spent many years as a witch before finding Christ as her Savior. She explained to me that in witchcraft, every one of Satan's teasers (drugs, rock music, immoral sex, etc.) were tools they used to get demons inside people so they could control them and eventually destroy them.

The lights went on. It was like a fourth of July fireworks show inside my brain.

I thought about the man in Mark 9:22 in the Bible. The

devils (demons) inside this man drove him into fire and water to try and kill him. He couldn't stop himself.

Teenager, when you play with Satan's teasers, you are playing with literal demons. You might think you can quit whenever you want, but you're in for a shock.

And once the devil gets his demons inside you, it will bring new meaning to the words "I Got Ya!"

No wonder Bob couldn't stop abusing children. The demons inside him drove him to do it. When he said he really didn't want to do it, he was telling the truth. When he said "something came over him," it was the demons rising up within him.

No wonder junkies don't quit popping drugs? **They can't!** The demons inside them won't let them! (We'll talk more about drugs in chapter 9.)

No wonder kids are mysteriously killing themselves. That explains why the teen suicide rate is going through the roof. (More on suicide in chapter 12.)

A lady wrote to Ann Landers with a very similar problem. She began torturing small animals as a child. Her uncontrollable sadistic behavior bothered her so much that she put off having a family. She feared those same urges would cause her to hurt her children.

This poor lady said she cried her eyes out when she tortured an animal and swore she'd never do it again.

But those horrible feelings came boiling back to the surface and drove her to repeat several terrible acts.

When she finally did have children, it happened again. When those feelings came over her, she "couldn't control them." Though she loved her daughter, she damaged her so badly, she is handicapped for life.

This lady told Ann she was living in hell. She hated herself and had considered suicide. The only conclusion she could come to was that she must be crazy.[1]

No, she isn't crazy. The demons inside her drove her to do things she didn't want to do. And she's not alone. Millions of teens around the world are being driven to do destructive things they really don't want to do.

That's why gruesome stories keep popping up in newspapers every day. Here is a portion of one such article:

> *A group of teenagers murdered one of their friends because they reportedly wanted to to get a thrill out of watching him die a slow, painful death. One of the teens allegedly looked down at the victim and said: 'Hey Keith. It was nothing personal. We just wanted to see somebody die.'*
>
> *According to testimony, the young man was hit several times, had his feet tied*

71

and was stabbed. Using a stick and a bandanna, the youths wound a rope around the victim's neck. One of the boys then twisted it like a tourniquet until his 'eyes started to bulge.' Another of the youths then held a piece of pipe over one of the victim's eyes and tried to shove it inside his skull.

Obviously, this is not normal behavior, even for cruel and heartless teenagers. Without doubt, these young men were demon possessed. The demons merely used these young men to carry out this disgusting and torturous murder so they could send another soul to hell. That's what the devil is really after.

I Got Ya

Once the devil gets his demons inside you, he's got ya, just like the song says. If you don't believe me, believe AC/DC; they're telling you the same thing. (Look at the lyrics at the beginning of this chapter.)

A 17-year-old boy shot and killed a 16-year-old class-mate in the hallway of their high school. He then killed himself. In a taped message, he said he might kill two or three others "just to mess up some lives."[2]

The devil will use rebellion, peer pressure and decep-tion to prime you, then he'll apply one of several tried and tested tools to get his demons inside you.

From there, the stairway to hell gets very painful.

Now you start to pay. Those "fun" things you used to enjoy now become a cruel master. Your laughter turns to crying. That arrogant smirk on your face vanishes like the setting sun. Reality sets in.

A 15-year-old boy was accused of stabbing his stepfather to death when he was asked to hang up the phone.[3]

Incidents like these are obviously not normal. And while "experts" search day and night for answers, the demons keep right on killing teens and sending them straight to hell.

Trapped

Don't plan on getting out or quitting once the demons enter you either. They won't let you. Now Satan's got ya. The rock stars tried to warn you. You should have listened.

What are some of Satan's favorite tools for getting demons inside teens? How about so-called "innocent" games like Dungeons and Dragons? What about drugs, rock music and sex? Are you in danger when you participate in any of these activities?

Get ready for a shock . . .

Chapter 8

Don't Mess With My Music

If you love rock music, the devil's bloody claws are already firmly wrapped around your neck. The longer you listen, the tighter his grip gets.

Almost every teen on the stairway to hell is addicted to Satan's music. Rock music is one of the devil's most widely used tools for getting his soul-destroying demons inside young people.

It's destroying teens by the millions.

Satan is so sure of his stranglehold over teens that he now openly brags in rock songs of the fiery fate that awaits those who indulge in his music and lifestyle.

And not only are young people listening, they are paying $10 to $20 and more for the privilege of hearing on cassette or C.D. that they are going to burn in hell.

Teenager, look at these lyrics. The rock stars who sing them are sold-out servants of Satan, "preaching" for their master. And what they are saying in the following songs is true!

For once, the father of lies is telling the truth! He wants you to burn in hell in an actual lake of fire! The rock star's job is to help get you there. Only a grossly deceived person would idolize and worship people who are leading them to hell.

In their 1988 song "Can I Play With Madness," Iron Maiden says:

> *"I screamed aloud to the old man*
> *I said don't lie, don't say you don't know*
> *I say you'll pay for your mischief*
> *In this world or the next*
> *Oh and then he fixed me with a freezing*
>   *glance*
> *And the hell fires raged in his eyes*
> ***He said do you want to know the truth***
>   ***son***
> ***I'll tell you the truth***
> ***Your soul's gonna burn in the lake of***
>   ***fire."***

Burn In Hell, by Twisted Sister

> *"Welcome to the abandoned land*
> *Come on in child, take my hand*
> *Here there's only one bill to pay*
> *There's just five words to say*
> *As you go down, down, down*
> ***You're gonna burn in Hell . . . "***

Diary of a Madman, by Ozzy Osbourne

"A sickened mind and spirit
The mirror tells me lies
Will he escape my soul or will he live
in me
Is he tryin' to get out or tryin' to
enter me . . ."

Ozzy already knows the answer to those questions. A few thousand demons already live inside his body. Now he wants to get a few of his "friends" inside of you.

Number Of The Beast, by Iron Maiden

"In the night the fires are burning bright
The ritual has begun
Satan's work is done . . .
I'm coming back
I will return
And I'll posses your body
And I'll make you burn . . ."

See You In Hell, by Grim Reaper

"Can I make you an offer
You can't refuse . . .
And you can come with me
To a place you know so well
I will take you to the very gates
of Hell . . ."

N.I.B. (Nativity In Black), by Ozzy Osbourne

> *"Now I have you with me*
> ***Under my power***
> *Our love grows stronger now*
> *With every hour*
> *Look into my eyes*
> *You'll see who I am*
> ***My name is Lucifer***
> ***Please take my hand.***"

A former rock music worshipper told me about an Ozzy concert he went to. Though his mind was sizzled on drugs, his heart nearly stopped when he turned around and saw a man wearing a black hooded robe standing behind the crowd with his arms outstretched. This shocked teen suddenly realized he was in the middle of a Satanic service.

Like vomit, the disgusting lyrics keep spewing out:

God Of Thunder, by KISS

> *"And I command you to kneel before the*
> *God of thunder*
> *And Rock & Roll*
> ***The spell you're under***
> ***Will slowly rob you of your virgin soul.***"

Here, KISS **commands** you to bow before the god of Rock & Roll, none other than Satan himself.

He also admits that those who are enslaved by his

music are under a Satanic spell that will destroy their souls. In other words, **you are going to burn in hell.**

Little Dolls, by Ozzy Osbourne

*"Tortured and flaming you give birth to
  Hell
Living a nightmare
It's a pity you'll pray for your death
But he's in no hurry*
***Demons and curses that play on your
  soul . . ."***

Inject The Venom, by AC/DC

*"Got no heart and
Feel no pain*
Take your soul *and
Leave a stain . . ."*

You don't have to believe me. These famous rockers are all screaming it at you. The purpose of rock music is to get demons inside you to destroy you and drive you to hell.

If you would just listen, the rock stars themselves are telling you that your involvement with rock music is literally filling your body with demons.

C.O.D., by AC/DC

*"Care Of The Devil
Care Of The Devil* ***in me*** *. . . "*

AC/DC again admit that demons live inside them on their song "Hell Ain't A Bad Place To Be:"

> " . . . Late at night
> Turn down the light . . .
> Round my heart
> Tearin' me apart
> **Got the Devil in me . . .** "

AC/DC couldn't say it any plainer. Rock stars readily admit that the devil and his demons live **inside** them. Guess what they want to do to you, young person.

The song, The Oath, by Mercyful Fate, is the actual oath of allegiance to Satan that is recited when a person becomes a Satanist. Look at the lyrics:

> "By the Symbol of the Creator,
> I swear henceforth to be
> A faithful Servant of his most puissant
>   Arch-Angel
> The Prince Lucifer
> Whom the Creator designated as His
>   Regent
> And Lord of this World. Amen.
>
> I deny Jesus Christ, the deceiver
> And I abjure the Christian Faith
> Holding in contempt all of it's Works
>
> As a Being now possessed of a human
>   Body

> *In this World I swear to give my full*
>   *Allegiance*
> *To it's lawful Master, to worship Him*
> *Our Lord Satan, and no other . . .*
>
> *I swear to give my Mind, my Body and*
>   *Soul unreservedly*
> *To the Furtherance of our Lord Satan's*
>   *Designs . . . "*

Every time a person sings those lyrics, they are renewing their total allegiance to Satan. If that doesn't open the door for demons to come marching into your body, please tell me what does.

Judas Priest says this about Satan in their song, "Devil's Child:"

> *"Oh no you're so damned wicked*
> *You got me by the throat*
> *Oh no gotcha claws stuck in me*
> *You never let me go*
> *I believe you're the devil . . . "*

The Joke's On You

Teenager, you may think it's your parents who don't understand, but the joke is really on you. You're the one who is being deceived and set up for the kill.

Led Zeppelin gives you another clue in their song, "No Quarter," from their album "Houses Of The Holy:"

> *"Walking side by side with death*
> *The devil mocks their every step . . . "*

Behind your back, your enemy, Satan, is having a great big belly laugh as you blindly worship the evil rock stars who are helping to destroy you. The fact that you bluntly ignore the advice of anyone who tries to warn you is solid proof that Satan's demons already control you. You're on your way down.

The song "Lust" by Piledriver says:

> *"Hell on fire*
> *Lust, desire*
> *The Devil wants to lick you*
> *The Devil wants to stick you*
> ***Wants your body***
> ***Wants your spirit . . . "***

Hundreds of other songs could be listed, but the message is always the same, teen . . . the devil wants you to burn in hell.

Backmasking

When you listen to the lyrics of these songs when played forward, they provide more than enough proof of Satan's desire to get demons inside your body. But just in case you still want more evidence, here are a few backmasked messages from some famous rock albums:

The song, In League With Satan, by Venom, from

their "Welcome To Hell" album, contains this chilling backmasked message:

> *"Satan!*
> *Raised in Hell. Raised in Hell.*
> ***I'm gonna burn your soul . . . "***

What more needs to be said when a famous rock group titles a song, In League With Satan, names an album, Welcome To Hell, and boldly declares that Satan is "gonna burn your soul . . . "?

The Grim Reaper album, Fear No Evil, has a backmask on the song "Final Scream" which says:

> ***"See you in Hell."***

Tragically, in most cases, these rock stars are exactly right. Millions of their fans will join them in hell. But they won't see each other because they will all be blazing in the never-ending flames.

The last album recorded by Bon Scott, former AC/DC lead singer, was "Highway To Hell." On the title cut, he screamed out his parting words, "I'm on the Highway to Hell . . ." Little did he know that he would die before the song did.

If we could pull Bon Scott from hell's flames for just one minute and ask him about the "Highway To Hell" now that he's reached his final destination, he would surely sing a different tune. But we can't. For Bon, it's too late.

Rock Fueled Every Evil Fire

George's life was the pits. He had been screaming down the stairway to hell at break-neck speed.

Taking drugs, dealing drugs, living on the streets, alcohol, illicit sex, filth, rebellion, crime, high school dropout, hate, his life was lower than a bag of stinking garbage.

Many times I heard him share his pitiful life story. Each time, it was obvious that his life (and problems) revolved around rock music. Though he started off with the "mellow stuff," he couldn't stop there.

Through his teenage years, the demons that entered him through rock music (just like they said they would) drove him step after step down the painful stairway to hell.

His first L.S.D. "trip" was at an Ozzy Osbourne concert. From there, his life continued to tumble downward. He had promised himself that he'd never touch a needle, but the demons drove him to do it. He couldn't stop himself.

Down, down, down he went. And rock music fueled every destructive step.

Though rock music had begun as "innocent and fun," it eventually took total control of his life and nearly destroyed him. More about George a little later.

"Don't Touch My Music"

If you want to prove that teenagers who are hooked on rock music are demon infested, just try to take their rock away from them.

Many things will cause a teenager's blood to boil, but mess with their music, and you have a war on your hands. Why? Because now you've got their demons riled up. When that happens, look out. There's no telling what the demons will drive them to do.

A 13-year-old mother from Osaka, Japan was so "obsessed" (another word for "possessed") with the Satanic Heavy Metal rockers, Iron Maiden, that she sold her newborn twin baby girls to buy tickets to an upcoming Iron Maiden concert.

The newspaper reported that when she was arrested, she was wearing a "baseball cap and T-shirt displaying the rock band's eerie, Satanic-like logo . . ." The article also said that her "belief in Iron Maiden is so strong, she threatened to kill herself unless she was allowed to wear her hat."

Is there any question that demons controlled this young girl?

Rock Leads To Murder

A one-time, all-American, studious, 14-year-old boy from New Jersey read a school paper his friend did on Satanism. Within weeks, the newspaper reported, "he became a defiant, hostile teen buried in library books on the **occult** and listening to **heavy metal music.**" The two always go hand-in-hand.

Police said the boy was "entranced" (another word for "possessed") by the occult when he stabbed his mother 12 times. He tried to kill his father and 10-year-old brother by setting their house on fire. Next he slit his throat and wrists with a Boy Scout knife and slumped dead on bloody snow in a neighbor's yard.

The boy's father said that all week his son had been singing a rock song "about blood and killing your mother." He said his son told a friend about a vision in which Satan came to him, wearing his face, and urged him to kill his family and preach Satanism.[1]

The demons that entered him through the music took over his body and mind (like they said they would) and drove him to murder his mother and himself. His soul was destroyed (like his rock gods promised).

Through their songs, they had slapped him right in the face with the truth, yet he still never saw it.

Family Axed To Death

Another equally disturbing blood bath took place in Minnesota. A 16-year-old, well-liked, straight-A student hacked his entire family to death with an ax. The victims included his father, his mother, his 14-year-old sister and his 9-year-old brother.

Why would a teen do something as sick as that? The article said the boy's dad was upset over "sexually explicit" rock music his son was listening to. The boy also liked "hard-core punk rock, including a group called Suicidal Tendencies."[2]

Satan deceived another one, and four more souls were blasted off into eternity. The boy's life is ruined, and he will never escape the nightmare of what the demons inside him drove him to do.

How sad that many millions of young people around the world think rock music is harmless, or just "the music of their generation."

Teenager, don't let Satan fool you. It's **his** music.

It is dangerous! It is deadly!

When you soak up Satan's music, you are playing with real demons! If you don't want to invite demons into your body, and follow the path already taken by the young people we've just talked about, **stay away from Satan's rock music.**

Chapter 9

I Can't "Just Say No" To Drugs

A great-sounding anti-drug program swept across America with the super-slick slogan . . .

. . . *"Just say no" to drugs.*

There was a problem, though. Millions of teens and adults alike would love nothing more than to "just say no." But they can't! No matter how hard they try or how badly they want to quit, they simply can't.

Is this another demonic problem? Do drugs open a doorway for demons to enter your body?

I have a copy of a letter from a young man who is now 25. When he was 18, he had a very frightening experience. He says in part:

> *"During a horrible experience with LSD, I had a shocking introduction to the spiritual realities of life. The devil was inside of me and quite systematically taking over control of my will. As I resisted the ever increasing pressure within me to*

take my control away . . . a voice inside of me kept saying, 'This time I will have you fully!' I was completely terrified! Somehow I knew that this was satan..."[1]

The demons that entered this young man through his LSD "trips" began talking to him. This is not uncommon. Many drug abusers hear voices, but most don't know they are the voices of demons.

Hard core Satanism is on the rise, and experts are continually finding drug abuse directly linked to this growing demon possession problem.

In her book, **The Hidden Dangers of The Rainbow**, Constance Cumbey exposes the false teachings of the Satanic New Age Movement. She reveals that New Agers view drugs as a "way to draft soldiers into the New Age army . . . " New Age leaders don't see drugs as a problem, but "tools for transformation."[2]

They sure are tools . . . tools to get demons inside young people. Drugs then transform them into blind servants of Satan.

Steve had a drug background, including LSD. One day, it hit! Right out of nowhere he had a "flashback" and lost total control of his mind. *Something* had taken over. Though he talked in vague religious terms, he could no longer read or understand his Bible and his walk with God stopped cold.

He "recovered" and began to make progress, but

soon another "flashback" hit. He went on like that for about two or three weeks. Eventually, he was admitted to a mental hospital. The last I heard, when a friend went to see him, he was drugged up and babbling about nothing, oblivious to the fact that bugs were crawling through his dirty, greasy hair.

What happened? He got too close to the truth so the demons that entered him through his drug use caused what people call a "flashback" and got him out of there. As far as I know, he may still be in that hospital.

Teenager, you can argue if you want to but when you take drugs, you open your body for demons to enter.

You may not believe it now, but someday you will. When you realize you've been tricked and you want to quit drugs, but the demons won't let you, then you'll believe it. Ask any junkie whose life has been destroyed by drugs. He'd quit in a second if he could.

You may be thinking, "I just smoke pot and I can quit any time I want, so I don't have to worry." Wrong! Every young person I've dealt with who got hooked on drugs started the same way . . . on pot.

Like we talked about earlier, Satan always makes it look like fun at first, but the bottom *always* falls out.

Not long ago I saw a former pro football player on T.V. He told about how he sold his most prized possessions, his two Superbowl rings, for drugs. Why didn't he just say no? The demons wouldn't let him.

Teenager, you may think you know what you are playing with when you welcome drugs into your life. But as the demons take over your body and mind, and you lose control, you'll find out you were wrong. Unfortunately for you, Satan's demons play for keeps. It's one mistake that just may be your last.

Mike grew up in a big city. He was introduced to drugs at a young age. He wanted to be "cool" and impress his friends. He couldn't see any danger since he was only smoking pot. After all, several studies had concluded that pot was harmless.

He had promised himself that he would never do anything more than pot. He wasn't going to be stupid like those dumb junkies out on the streets.

As he continued his new-found lifestyle, several changes gradually took place in his life:

* *He grew more rebellious and his relationship with his mother fell apart.*
* *His interest in school dwindled and his grades tumbled.*
* *Rock music gradually became the controlling force in his life.*

Please understand, all this did not happen overnight. It took a long time. The change was so gradual, Mike never noticed how much he was changing.

Eventually, the demons that entered his body through the drugs began running his life. They drove him to do things he really didn't want to do:

* * He quit school, though he really wanted to go to college.
* * He moved up to stronger and stronger drugs, though he had promised himself he never would.
* * He began mugging people and stealing from stores to buy drugs.

His life was a non-stop downhill roller coaster ride. He went on to become a hopeless junkie, poking dirty needles into his collapsing veins, living for that next high, hoping he wouldn't overdose and die.

The demons now totally ruled his life. He shared rooms with rats and ate slop out of garbage cans. He bounced in and out of jails, his criminal record growing like mold on a piece of stale bread.

When he was desperate for a fix, he even lowered himself to selling his body to perverted and deviate men as a homosexual prostitute.

Why didn't he just quit drugs? Because he couldn't! The demons wouldn't let him. They had sucked him in and slowly wrapped the noose around his neck. Now they had him. His hopes for the future were gone! His career dreams. Gone! His happiness. Gone! His mind. Gone! Everything. Gone!

How those demons must have laughed years ago when this poor young man promised himself that he would never take anything stronger than pot. He had no idea what he was playing with. And he sure didn't know that he was racing head-long down a carefully planned stairway to hell.

Teenager, don't believe the devil's lie that quitting drugs is as easy as just saying no. Once your body is infested with demons, you will do things you never dreamed you would. And ultimately, you will be dragged, just like Mike, straight down the devil's misery-filled stairway.

Have you ever wondered why so many teens kill themselves while high on drugs? Now you know. The demons get them high, take control of their bodies, then drive them to kill themselves.

Presto. Another soul burning in the lake of fire. The demons pat themselves on the back, congratulate each other on a job well done, and begin work on their next victim. Maybe you!

If thoughts like, "he's crazy" or "he doesn't know what he's talking about" are flooding into your mind right now, be careful. Those thoughts are coming straight from your arch enemy, the devil. He does not want you to know his real purpose for drugs.

Don't let him fool you any longer, young person.

Drugs aren't Satan's only weapon, though. He has several others that you need to know about. Let's look at another one . . .

Chapter 10

D & D: Just a Game?

The devil is using many different tools today to trick young people into riding the fast lane down the stairway to hell.

One of the most dangerous and widespread of all those tools is his fantasy role playing game, Dungeons and Dragons.

Literally millions of young people are unknowingly participating in genuine occult practices and opening the doors for demons to enter their bodies through this seemingly innocent game.

By the time they find out they were hood-winked, it's too late. They have taken that last step down the stairway to hell and are greeted by the engulfing flames.

Here are just a few who have seen first hand what hell is really like because they fell for this dangerous deception:

Murder – Suicide

Daniel (16) and his brother Stephen (14) died together in a D & D "murder — suicide." Stephen shot and killed his brother, then turned the weapon and used it on himself.

Authorities are convinced their deaths were related to D & D. The local Police Detective who handled the case, came to this conclusion about the two brutal deaths:

> *"There is no doubt that D & D cost them their lives."*[1]

Murdered Four People

Daniel sat in a Kansas jail cell after a crime spree that left four dead and four others wounded. When a reporter visited his cell and asked about his motives for the killings, he replied:

> *"Have you ever heard of Dungeons and Dragons? That had a lot to do with it."*
> *He added, "It's not just a board game, it's a lot deeper than a board game."*[2]

The youth also said he had five friends who were "locked up for the same thing right now (because of the game)."

A retired police officer who lectures police groups on the occult said D & D is:

" . . . supposed to be a board game, but kids play it for life and death on the street. "[3]

Strangled Two Children To Death

The headline read, "Boy was driven to kill." A 14-year-old boy who "loved playing the fantasy game Dungeons and Dragons" admitted strangling a 9-year-old girl and her 11-year-old brother.

Under hypnosis, the young murderer recalled seeing the boy "with a rope around his throat, purple, bleeding, struggling, falling to the floor."

The director of a local mental health clinic testified that the boy "became obsessed (a nice way of saying possessed) with the sudden need to kill." A psychiatrist agreed that the boy was "suddenly obsessed with killing." According to testimony, the boy killed "coolly, as if he were a spectator, and with no feeling."[4]

What happened? How could a 14-year-old child murder two young children in cold blood for no reason and with no feeling? Simple. He had been playing Dungeons and Dragons for a year and a half and had been a dungeon master for 5 months.

Through D & D, the demons entered his body and drove him to commit the murders.

Did you notice that this child became "obsessed" with

the sudden need to kill? That doesn't describe a normal (or even abnormal) 14-year-old. That describes a boy who is possessed by demons.

The newspaper reported that the child killer said he felt like a "spectator" at the killings. That's because he was. It was Satan's evil demons who were interested in killing those innocent children, not the boy. Since they completely controlled him, they drove him to kill those children. He was just a human vessel the demons used to kill two more precious lives.

This poor boy really was a bystander. But because he was deceived, it will haunt him for the rest of his life.

How did the demons get in him? Through the D & D. That's the ultimate (but well hidden) purpose of the "game." When a player begins worshiping a new deity (Satan) and asking help of characters in the game (demons), they are doing exactly what out-and-out Satan worshipers do, they just don't realize it.

Around the world, teens and adults are opening the door for demons to enter their bodies through D & D. The heartbreaking part is that they have no idea what's happening to them.

If you are a D & D player, Satan's plans for you are the same as the youngsters we've just listed. Before you say it will never happen to you, do you suppose any of these teens thought they would become cold blooded murderers while still in their teens?

Satan has deceived you just like he deceived them. You're on the stairway to hell and don't even know it. That's just the way Satan wants to keep it.

You say, "I don't believe D & D has anything to do with Satan or religion." Then let's turn to page 25, paragraph 3 of "Deities and Demigods (instruction manual) and see what D & D says about itself.

> *"Serving a deity is a significant part of D & D, and all players should have a patron god."*[5]

Surprise D & D player! Guess which deity you are serving? Satan! The list of deceived victims of this deadly demonic "game" never stops:

Suicide

A 16-year-old active D & D player shot himself through the heart just hours after a D & D curse was placed on him during a D & D game at his high school.[6]

Murdered His Father

A 17-year-old boy from Wisconsin murdered his foster father after becoming "obsessed (there's that word again) with playing D & D." At his trial it was revealed that he played D & D "several hours per day," and had reached a "high level of expertise."

Three months before the murder, he wrote one of his

D & D playing buddies that this would be his last letter "because I will probably be in jail for (first) and (second) degree murder and arson. This is no joke."[7]

In his book, "None Dare Call It Witchcraft," Dr. Gary North describes D & D as:

> " . . .the most effective, most magnifi-cently packaged, most thoroughly re-searched introduction to the occult in man's recorded history."[8]

I remember talking with a desperate boy who had played D & D for several years. Though it started as just a game, it didn't stay that way for long.

To progress in the game, he asked D & D "creatures" to help him win battles. He had no idea, but those creatures were literal demons. When he asked them to come to him and help him, he was unknowingly in-viting actual demons into his body.

As he got deeper and deeper into the game, fear began to overtake him. He eventually caught on that he was into more than what he bargained for. It was then he decided to quit the "game."

When he started talking about quitting, he began hearing voices in his head. The demons inside him threatened to kill him if he stopped playing the game.

The last time I saw him, he admitted becoming pos-sessed with demons through D & D. He also confessed that the demons now controlled his entire life. He was terrified! He feared that remaining in the game would lead to his death, and trying to get out would bring the same fate.

If only he had known all that before he let some of his friends persuade him to play D & D for the first time. Satan counted on his ignorance, and won.

He's counting on your ignorance too!

Official Investigation

To find out if D & D used authentic occult materials, the CBN television network assigned an investigator to study the question. He appeared on a CBN interview, along with a former employee of the company that makes D & D to announce their findings.

They concluded that D & D does contain authentic occult materials. Rituals, magic spells, charms, names of demons, etc. were all **authentic**. They said a list of names of demons and devils that were in a new D & D book kept showing up in the Bible.

The conclusion of the study should send shivers up and down the spine of every D & D playing teenager. They found that D & D is *"not fantasy."*[9]

Shot Himself In The Head

The parents of a 17-year-old boy watched their son calling up D & D demons only moments before he took his own life by shooting himself in the head.[10]

Suicide By Auto-Erotic Hanging

Before ending his own life, an 18-year-old boy from Marion, Ohio was noted to be "possessed (there it is again) by D & D as though he were living the game."[11]

Murdered by Two D & D Friends

An 18-year-old girl was murdered by two friends with whom she played D & D frequently. The killers were heavily into D & D. The victim was bound and gagged and died by strangulation.[12]

One last grizzly story.

Murdered Both Parents and A Clerk

Sean, 17, was found guilty of first-degree murder for shooting both his parents and a convenience store clerk. He supposedly shot the clerk to see what it felt like, then shot both his parents in their sleep so he could do whatever he wanted.

After the verdict was announced, Sean told reporters that he wanted to warn other youth about satanism, the occult and "Dungeons and Dragons."

> *"I want to warn teenagers who are out there. It's not the way. It's not the way. Jesus is the only answer that's out there . . . and it's time teenagers got serious*

*about Jesus here in America. It's time
now."*

Sean said he didn't remember if he killed his parents.

*"I loved my parents" he cried out. "And
if something like this — satanism and
'Dungeons and Dragons' could have
caused me to do something like this.
Think, people, think."*[13]

Once he had been tricked into the occult through D
& D, Sean's satanic beliefs led him to recruit his
friends to form a coven, drink blood during rituals and
pledge to "serve only Satan" in a blood pact.

According to official court testimony, Sean, an expe-
rienced D & D player, told a friend that he saw flying
demons when he prayed to Satan.

During the trial, an attorney read a tear-jerking letter
Sean's mother had written to her son just hours before
he brutally murdered her. In it, she wrote of her love
for him and her desire to help him. Part of the letter
read:

*"My son, my son, I see so much pain, so
much anger. How can I help you?"*

Sean wept as his attorney read the letter. What happened? Two parents loved their son and he loved
them. Yet he brutally blew their brains out while they
slept . . . all for no reason. Why?

D & D provided the doorway for demons to enter the body of this unsuspecting teenager, which led to full blown Satan worship. Then the demons, totally controlling him, drove him to murder the two people who loved him more than anyone else.

What a tragedy! And in his own words, Sean admits that it was all caused by his participation in Dungeons and Dragons.

Many teenagers have committed suicide when their D & D character died. Others have murdered friends, parents and others because they played the "game." Rapes, tortures and untold other gruesome and sick crimes have also been linked to D & D.

Teenager, before you play your first game of D & D, ask yourself:

> *"Do I want to invite real demons into my life so they can do to me what they did to Sean and the others we've talked about?"*

If your answer is no, then stay away from D & D!

Dungeons and Dragons is one of Satan's sneakiest tactics, leading a long parade of unsuspecting souls down the stairway to hell.

If you want to stay off that deadly stairway, steer clear of Dungeons and Dragons.

Chapter 11

What's Wrong With Sex?

Sex.

One of the hottest issues for teenagers today.

It causes so many problems:

* *Risk of getting AIDS*
* *Risk of herpes or other venereal diseases*
* *Unwanted pregnancies*
* *Abortions*
* *Emotional problems*
* *Raging debates with parents*
* *On and on it goes . . .*

But, teenager, there is another problem with pre-marital sex, and it's more important than all the others put together.

And chances are, you don't even know about it.

What is it? Let's see . . .

When it comes to sex, the devil has done another superb job of confusing the issue and shifting blame that belongs on his shoulders onto the shoulders of God.

Thanks to Satan's hard work, many young people think of God as a mean, old-fashioned, kill-joy who hates sex and is always against it, viciously punishing anyone who dares to enjoy it.

Satan, on the other hand, is portrayed as a real great guy. "If it feels good, do it" is his motto. "Enjoy sex. Go ahead . . . it's fun."

Let's sort out the lies, look at some facts, and see how Satan is using illicit sex to send deceived teens tumbling down the stairway to hell.

God Is Not Against Sex

First, sex is not bad and God is not against all sex. That's one of Satan's biggest lies. From the very beginning, God created sex for his creations to enjoy and placed his stamp of approval on it.

> *"So God created man in his own image, in the image of God created he him; male and female created he them. And God blessed them, and God said unto them, Be fruitful, and multiply, and replenish the earth. . . "*   *Genesis 1: 27-28*

But sex is not good for everyone. Here's where you

have to keep your eyes on the sly old devil. He's about to pull a fast one on you.

God, in His never-ending love and wisdom, created sex for married couples to enjoy. For them, it is a blessed and beautiful act, strengthening their marriage and tightening the bond of love between them.

The Bible plainly teaches this truth:

> *"Let thy fountain be blessed: and rejoice with the wife of thy youth. Let her be as the loving hind and pleasant roe; let her breasts satisfy thee at all times; and be thou ravished always with her love."*
> *Proverbs 5:18-19*

God went on in Genesis 2:24 to say:

> *"Therefore shall a man leave his father and mother, and shall cleave (be joined together) unto his wife: and they shall be one flesh."*

> *"Marriage is honourable in all, and the bed undefiled . . . "* *Hebrews 13:4*

God created sex for married couples to enjoy. For them, it is perfectly acceptable in God's sight.

But God did not create sex for those who are not married to each other. For them, it is deadly, both physically and spiritually.

Because God loves you and wants no harm to come to you, He has written stern warnings about becoming sexually active outside the bounds of marriage. Throughout the Bible, God clearly spells out what will happen to those who disregard His instructions about the misuse of sex.

> *"Now the works of the flesh are manifest, which are these; **Adultery, fornication**, uncleanness, lasciviousness . . . Envyings, murders, drunkenness, revellings, and such like: of the which I tell you before, as I have also told you in time past, that they which do such things **shall not inherit the kingdom of God."***
> *Galatians 5:19,21*

> *"But the fearful, and unbelieving, and the abominable, and murderers, and **whoremongers (fornicators)**, and sorcerers, and idolaters, and all liars, **shall have their part in the lake which burneth with fire and brimstone:** which is the second death."*   *Revelation 21:8*

Over and over, the unmistakable message rings out. Disobey God's laws regarding sex and the devil will see that you descend every step on the stairway to hell and burn in the eternal lake of fire.

> *"Know ye not that the unrighteous shall **not** inherit the kingdom of God? Be not deceived: neither **fornicators**, nor idola-*

> tors, nor **adulterers**, nor effeminate, nor
> **abusers of themselves with mankind.**
> Nor thieves, nor covetous, nor drunk-
> ards, nor revilers, nor extortioners, shall
> inherit the kingdom of God."
> I Corinthians 6:9-10

Here's where Satan pulls his fast one. While God is trying to warn you by saying, "Don't do it, it will destroy you," the devil is taunting you, saying, "Go ahead, it will be great."

What the devil isn't telling you is that through illicit sex you will open the door for demons to enter your body and destroy you.

The Bible gives this crystal clear warning:

> "But whoso committeth adultery with a
> woman lacketh understanding: he that
> doeth it **destroyeth his own soul.**"
> Proverbs 6:32

Most teenagers don't know that sexual contact with their girlfriend or boyfriend opens the doorway for demons to enter them. They are actually helping Satan destroy their souls and damn them to an eternity in hell.

Teenager, God doesn't want that to happen to you. Look at this warning in II Peter 2:19:

> "While they promise them liberty, they

themselves are the servants of corruption: for of whom a man is overcome, of the same is he brought in bondage."

That sounds like today, doesn't it? Teens are being promised liberty everywhere they turn. But the ones doing the promising are the servants of corruption (Satan). And, teen, once you give in to the temptation, you will be brought under Satan's bondage.

A wise father gives this good advice to his son:

> *"For the lips of a strange woman drop as an honeycomb, and her mouth is smoother than oil: But her end is bitter as wormwood, sharp as a twoedged sword. Her feet go down to death; her steps take hold on hell . . . Remove thy way far from her, and come not nigh (near) the door of her house: Lest thou . . . mourn at the last, **when thy flesh and thy body are consumed . . .** "*
> *Proverbs 5:3-5,8,11*

The Bible promises that Satan and his demons will consume your flesh and your body if you give in to the fleshly desires for sex outside of marriage.

Teenager, you are playing with fire . . . and you **will** get burned. Before your next sexual encounter, ask yourself this question:

> *"Am I willing to allow Satan and his de-*

*mons to consume my flesh and body, de-
stroy my soul, and condemn me to burn
in a literal lake of fire, in exchange for
these few minutes of pleasure?"*

That's the decision you must make! Millions of young
people have risked everything for a few sweaty lust-
filled minutes, hoping God's promises would not come
to pass. They all found out the hard way that God
wasn't kidding. For that mistake, they will pay dearly
forever.

Remember teen, immoral sex always brings ruin and
damnation. Don't fall into this very seductive Satanic
trap.

And don't get mad at God for giving you rules about
sex. He knows that sex outside marriage will destroy
you, so He's warned you against it to try and save you
from suffering.

The one you should be furious with is the devil. He's
the seedy character who's trying to get you to become sexually active before marriage. He wants to
get his demons inside you so he can destroy your
body and soul.

The Bible gives you another warning about sex:

*"What? know ye not that he which is
joined to an harlot is one body? for two,
saith he, shall be one flesh . . . Flee
fornication. Every sin that a man doeth*

*is without the body; but he that commit-
teth fornication sinneth against his own
body."*   *I Corinthians 6:16,18*

God gave you these warning about having sex before marriage because He loves you and He doesn't want your life to be destroyed.

Homosexuality

While we're on the subject of sex, you need to know about another of your enemy's darkest and most deviate secrets . . . homosexuality.

There is nothing quite as sad as a young person who is enslaved in the bondage of this unnatural and perverted lifestyle. Like a fly squirming to break out of a web when he is about to be a spider's lunch, teens, once caught in the devilish web of homosexuality, are powerless to escape.

The heartbreaking tragedy is that many young people are sucked into this demonic trap against their will at a very young age. But regardless of the beginning, the result is always the same.

Teenager, be warned. When you experiment with homosexuality or lesbianism, you are playing with demons. God has hated this wicked lifestyle from the beginning of time. Back in Old Testament times, He gave this command:

"If a man also lie with mankind, as he

> *lieth with a woman, both of them have committed an abomination (something extremely disgusting to God): they shall surely be put to death;" Leviticus 20:13*

In the book of Romans, we learn more about the demonic infestation of homosexuals:

> *"Wherefore God also gave them up to uncleanness through the lusts of their own hearts, to dishonour their own bodies between themselves: For this cause God gave them up unto vile affections . . . And likewise also the men, leaving the natural use of the woman, burned in their lust one toward another; men with men working that which is unseemly (indecent or shameful) . . . And even as they did not like to retain God in their knowledge, God gave them over to a reprobate mind, to do those things which are not convenient (fitting) . . . Who knowing the judgment of God, that they which commit such things are worthy of death, not only do the same, but have pleasure in them that do them."*
> Romans 1:24-28,32

Several things here:

1. God "gave them up." The demons within them had such total control of their minds and bodies that God completely gave up on them.

115

2. God "gave them over to a reprobate mind." Satan had complete control of their minds. Teenager, homosexuality is not just a harmless "alternate lifestyle;" it is a cruel and heartless weapon used by Satan to gain control of the minds, bodies and souls of its victims.

3. Though they knew the penalty for this unnatural use of their bodies, even that didn't make these men change their wicked ways. In fact, they not only continued, they actually had pleasure in their perverted lifestyle.

What a slap in God's face. The only way anyone could find joy and pleasure from that kind of unnatural sex act is to be driven 100 percent by demons.

I remember a very emotional and highly confidential letter from a young man who got trapped in the web of homosexuality several years earlier. He confessed that it was a miserable, rotten lifestyle. He wanted out, but couldn't quit. He hated it, but couldn't stop.

He urged us to do everything we could to discourage other teens from making the same tragic mistake he did . . . becoming involved in homosexuality.

In a nutshell, his letter confirmed that homosexuality is another way demons enter your body, and another well hidden step down the lust-filled stairway to hell. God says it very plainly. All homosexuals will anguish in the red-hot flames of hell forever:

*"Be not deceived: neither fornicators, nor idolaters, nor adulterers, nor effeminate (feminine men), **nor abusers of themselves with mankind (homosexuals)** . . . shall inherit the kingdom of God."*
I Corinthians 6:9-10

How much plainer could it be? God calls out to you, **"Be not deceived."** Obviously, he knew Satan would try to deceive you on this matter. Homosexuals "shall **not** inherit the kingdom of God."

There's no debate about it. If you don't agree, take it up with God; He wrote it. I'm just telling you what He said. Though many don't want to believe it, homosexuality is a one-way ticket that leads straight to hell.

Sexual Perversion

Another powerful proof that illicit sex causes demons to enter your body is the long list of deviate sexual perversions that have followed our liberal attitudes about sex.

Once sexual demons move into your body, they will never be satisfied, no matter how much or what type of sex they get you to perform. They will continually drag you to new disgusting lows. You will do things you never dreamed you would.

One young man started off having sex with his girlfriend, but it didn't stop there. (It never does when Satan sinks his blood-sucking fangs in you.) The de-

117

mons eventually drove him to the wretched life of a homosexual prostitute.

I could tell you the stories of hundreds and hundreds of others who thought that having sex wouldn't hurt anything. But it almost always seemed to get perverted. Some of the stories I've heard would curl your toe nails.

"Snuff" Films

Business is booming these days for the producers of movies called "snuff films."

When the director yells "action," the cameras roll and the sexual perversion begins. The "star" of the film is tied down. Others then begin beating and torturing her. After a variety of perverted sex acts are performed, they draw razor-sharp knives and slowly slice off her arms and legs.

As blood runs everywhere, sexually aroused viewers are delighted. There is no limit to the torture. Eyes might be gouged out, faces slashed, sex organs cut off . . . the sicker the better.

Eventually, the "star" is murdered. Once she is dead, the director bellows out, "cut!" Another best seller "in the can." Unbelievably, these films are in incredibly high demand. People are paying fortunes for them. Once you give the demons an open doorway into your life, there is no limit. Look at the perverted sexual activities people are enslaved by these days:

1. Sex with animals
2. Sex with dead bodies
3. Sex with children
4. Snuff films
5. Sadomasochism
6. Incest
7. Homosexuality
8. Lesbianism

These sickening and degrading acts scream out that demons are controlling and driving deceived victims to perform some of the sickest acts imaginable.

Teenager, immoral sex will lead to your ruin. It is a tool of Satan to get you and keep you traveling down the stairway to hell.

And it will start off looking very innocent and harmless. It always does at first. But what you don't know is that hot Friday night with your boyfriend or girlfriend opened the floodgates for demons to come pouring into your life.

Stop and think about it right now. If you don't want want demons entering and controlling you, don't open the door through sex before marriage.

Chapter 12

Suicide's Not The Solution

Have you ever thought about taking your life, teen?

If you have, you can be sure of one thing . . .

. . . Satan and his demons have been working you over.

Plain and simple, the devil wants you dead! He's licking his chops and grinning from ear to ear just thinking about watching your flesh sizzling in the eternal flames of hell.

And he wants it to happen . . . now!

You are not the only young person he wants dead, though. The statistics on teenage suicides are sky-rocketing.

The devil's plan is working perfectly. First he plants demons inside teens through rock music, drugs and other means. Then, step by step, helpless youngsters are dragged down to the bottom of Satan's stairway.

The demons then drive those teens to a suicide attempt.

No matter what you've heard about suicide, understand this: suicide is the last step down the stairway to hell and it leads straight to everlasting damnation.

During my work with troubled teens, I've heard about many teenagers who committed suicide for some really ridiculous reasons:

* *One young boy's suicide note said he had killed himself because his acne problem was more than he could stand.*

* *Because his girlfriend broke up with him, another teen pulled a pistol out of a drawer and blew his brains out.*

The list goes on and on. Obviously, no right-thinking person would kill himself for reasons like these.

Then why? Why the big increase in teen suicides over the last few years? Demons are driving teens to take their own lives . . . and the poor young people have no idea what hit them.

Advertising

Another big reason for the radical increase in teen suicides is greatly increased advertising. Every place you turn, Satan is advertising and promoting suicide as the solution to the problems of young people.

Ozzy Osbourne's song, "Suicide Solution," was not written by accident. Every word came directly from Ozzy's evil master. A teenager blew his brains out with a .38 revolver after continuously listening to Ozzy's dangerously demonic death march. The song was still playing when the police found the body.

Many other rock songs tell impressionable young teens that suicide is the answer. Tragically, teens are listening.

Two teenage boys made a suicide pact after listening to a Judas Priest album. One boy succeeded; the other survived, but without his face.[1]

Read these satanic lyrics from "Suicidal Tendencies":

Suicidal Failure

"Father forgive me
For I know not what I do
I tried everything
Now I'll leave it up to you
I don't want to live
I don't know why
I don't have no reason
I just want to die."

Memories Of Tomorrow

"Mass starvation, Contaminated water
Destroyed cities, Mutilated bodies
I'll kill myself. I'd rather die.

If you could see the future
You'd know why."

Suicide's An Alternative

"Sick of people - no one real
Sick of chicks - they're all bitches
Sick of you - you're too hip
Sick of life - it sucks . . .
Sick of life, it sucks;
Sick and tired - and no one cares;
Sick of myself - don't wanna live;
Sick of living - gonna die."

AC/DC pushes suicide in their song, "Shoot To Thrill."
At least one fan took their deadly advice. A teen shot
and killed himself while playing the song on his Walk-
man.

Blue Oyster Cult's "Don't Fear The Reaper" tells teens
that dying and going to hell is nothing to be afraid of:

"Come on baby (Don't fear the reaper)
Baby take my hand (Don't fear the
* reaper)*
We'll be able to fly (Don't fear the reaper)"

There are many other vehicles Satan is using to push
his favorite product:

Public school students are being forced to
attend actual suicide classes.

T. V. is another of his favorite outlets. The theme song for the long-running T. V. show MASH was "Suicide Is Painless."

Movies also provide great advertising. In the movie, Better Off Dead, the main character keeps trying to find new ways to kill himself. Whenever he has a problem, his answer is a suicide attempt. Though it was supposed to be funny, I doubt that parents whose teens have killed themselves saw the humor in it.

I'm Glad I Failed

There is one sure proof that almost all teenage suicides are motivated by demons. I have counselled with hundreds of teens who have tried to end it all. I could not tell you how many times I heard stories like:

"As soon as I swallowed all the pills, I realized I really didn't want to die. I couldn't believe what I had just done. I started fighting to live." Another teen said:

"I thought I wanted to end it all, but right after I slit my wrists, I did everything I could to stop the bleeding. I knew I didn't want to die."

What happens? The demons within young people drive them to try and kill themselves. Suicide is the demon's goal, not the young person's.

Once the suicide attempt has been made, the teen-ager realizes what has happened and immediately begins fighting for his life. He does not want to die.

Here is a typical example:

Carol couldn't take any more. Her parents were always on her back. Drugs were clouding her mind and changing her attitudes about life.

She hated living at home, but had nowhere else to go. She had just broken up with her boyfriend and felt very alone. Depression was crushing her.

Her school grades dropped and a veil of darkness fell over her, pushing all light from her life. She was about to explode under the pressure. She had nothing left to live for. She knew what she had to do.

She snuck into the bathroom one night, grabbed a bottle of bleach and guzzled it down. Before gulping down the last drop, she came to her senses.

"What have I done? I don't want to die," she cried out!

Grabing the phone, she called an ambulance. "Help! I'm gonna die! Please come quick!" She then screamed to her parents, "Help, I need help!"

Within minutes her stomach was being pumped at the hospital. All the time she was weeping and praying,

"Oh, God, please don't let me die!"

Did this girl really want to die? No way! It was Satan who wanted her to drop off the last step of the stairway to hell and into the burning flames.

No Second Chance

Bill was not as lucky. When he decided to end his life, he snuck a shotgun up to his bedroom. After loading the weapon and sticking the gun barrel in his mouth, he pulled the trigger. He got no second chance.

Within seconds, parts of his body were scattered all across the room. Worse, he went straight to hell, where he will burn forever.

I remember seeing a videotape of a boy who tried to kill himself like Bill did. He crammed the barrel of a shotgun in his mouth and pulled the trigger. Though he blew off most of his face, he didn't die. He now warns teens that suicide's not the answer.

Teenager, suicide is *not*, I repeat, *not* the solution to your problems. When thoughts of killing yourself creep into your mind, there is no doubt about it, Satan and his wicked demons are trying to shove you off the stairway to hell's last fatal step.

No matter how painful your problems are, they are nothing compared to the eternal torture that is awaiting you in hell.

Don't let Satan deceive you. Suicide will not solve your problems, it will seal your doom in hell.

Chapter 13

Satan Worship: The Ultimate Deception

One of Satan's biggest laughs must be over all the teens he has tricked world-wide into joining literal Satan worship groups.

It is no secret that Satan worship is spreading like drugs at a rock concert. Tens of thousands of teens are willingly joining Satanic covens.

With promises of power, fame and friends, teens are pledging their lives to outright service of Satan.

Here are some enticing offers you will hear when Satan's workers try to convince you to pledge your allegiance to their master:

* *"You can have any girl or any guy you want."*

* *"You can have all the drugs and money you want."*

* *"You can be the most popular person in school."*

* *"You can have power to control other people."*

* *"Whatever your little heart desires, you can have it."*

Sounds great, doesn't it? That's why hundreds of thousands of teens are giving their lives to Satan.

You Forgot To Tell Me About This Part

But there's another side to devil worship, a side your enemy, Satan, keeps well hidden from you until you are past the point of no return.

Once you've been recruited, Satan's first job is to get his demons inside you. Once he does that, the party's over. Now you are trapped! You can't quit, even if you want to. You are powerless to help yourself.

Satan now has total control of you. All you can do is stand by and helplessly endure the misery and agony your evil master has planned for you.

Let's look at some teenagers just like you and see how devil worship turned out for them after they believed the devil's lies and swore to serve only him:

> *In Montana, a Satan worshiper stabbed a man 27 times, cut off his arms and legs, carved out his heart and ate it. He had one of the man's fingers in his pocket when he was arrested.*[1]

In Massachusetts, a Satanic cult killed a 20-year-old woman, cut off her fingers, slit her throat, and chopped her head off and kicked it around. The leader then had sex with the decapitated and mutilated dead body.[2]

I wonder why Satanists never mention these kinds of activities to prospective members before they join up. Here are a few more examples:

Ten straight-A teenagers in an Ontario, California high school recently put together a step by step plan on how to get rid of their parents. Step 10 was to be the "ultimate sacrifice," cutting up the parents' bodies and feeding them to dogs, then sacrificing the dogs.[3]

A 17-year-old boy was tied to a bed as part of a satanic ritual. Four Satan worshippers then poured lighter fluid on him, taped firecrackers to his body and urinated on him while reciting a satanic chant. The helpless young man was then set on fire. The Satanists videotaped the entire event so they could "enjoy" it over and over.[4]

After pledging his allegiance to Satan, Richard Ramirez went on to live a life very pleasing to his master. He was arrested and charged with 14 brutal nighttime murders and 54 other felonies, including sex-

*ual attacks, robberies and burglaries. In a
packed court room at his trial, he proudly
flashed a pentagram (Satanic symbol) and
shouted "Hail Satan!"*[5]

There's Still More

There are other required activities Satanists forget to
mention when they're enticing you to join. Satan worshipers are forced to drink stuff like urine and blood.
They perform all kinds of bloody animal sacrifices in
their rituals. But it doesn't stop there.

Experts estimate that between 50,000 and 60,000
satanic human sacrifices take place every year in the
United States alone.[6] That's 170 human sacrifices
every single day. Their favorite victims are babies;
the younger the better.

If you're real smart, you've already figured out that
they need 50,000 to 60,000 victims every year. Once
you've joined, you just may get "volunteered."

Writing on teen satanism, Lisa Levitt Ryckman says:

> *"The ultimate thing you can do in satanic
> worship is kill yourself. It's the highest
> tribute to Satan."*[7]

Of course it's the highest tribute to Satan. It fulfills his
ultimate goal, deceiving you into taking the last step
down the stairway to hell so you can burn with him
forever in the lake of fire.

In New Zealand, the newspaper headline read, **"Three Rock Fans Die In 'Devil' Pack."** Teens who worship satanic rock groups like "Sisters of Mercy" and "Jesus and Mary Chain" are killing themselves in cult related suicide pacts. A 16-year-old boy blasted himself through the head with a .22 rifle. Two other 16-year-olds died in cars filled with exhaust fumes.[8]

Don't Be Deceived

Why would any teenager (or adult, for that matter) join a group with activities like this? One very simple reason . . . because they've been horribly deceived.

Today, Satan is deceiving and destroying teens like never before. They are swallowing his lies and blindly stumbling down his agony-filled steps, blindly serving the one who is planning their eternal torment.

While they search for the lust-filling teasers Satan promised them, their lives are being destroyed. As they dream big dreams, they tumble and slide closer and closer to those red-hot scorching flames.

Teenager, Satan will promise you the world. And to be very honest, there are a lot of things he can give you. But don't ever forget, those material things will never be worth it when you begin paying for them, both in this life and while you burn forever in hell.

Doomed To Hell

Because of his pride and rebellion against God, Satan

was doomed to spend eternity burning in the lake of fire since before the creation of the world. Look what Almighty God said:

> *"How art thou fallen from heaven, O Lucifer, son of the morning! how art thou cut down to the ground, which didst weaken the nations!*

> *"For thou hast said in thine heart, I will ascend into heaven, I will exalt my throne above the stars of God: I will sit also upon the mount of the congregation, in the sides of the north: I will ascend above the heights of the clouds; I will be like the most High. **Yet thou shalt be brought down to hell, to the sides of the pit."***   *Isaiah 14:12-15*

Satan's last stop is in hell . . . and it won't be a party:

> *"And the devil that deceived them was cast into the lake of fire and brimstone, where the beast and the false prophet are, **and shall be tormented day and night for ever and ever."***
> *Revelation 20:10*

Satan knows where he's headed and he knows the everlasting punishment that awaits him there. Now he wants to persuade everyone he can (including you) to follow him to that place of torment.

He'll make you believe any of his lies that he can to deceive you into being his roommate in hell forever.

* *If he can make you believe that you will rule and reign with him there, then he'll do that.*

* *If he can make you believe that hell doesn't really exist, then that's what he'll do.*

* *If he can convince you that hell is a wonderful place, that will be his tactic.*

Satan will do whatever it takes to stop you from believing and receiving the truth. And the truth is; Satan hates you with a passion! His only desire is to hear your agonizing screams as you share his torture in the burning flames of hell.

The Father of Lies

The devil has always been a master deceiver and a master liar. Look what the Bible says about him:

> *"Ye are of your father the devil, and the lusts of your father ye will do. He was a murderer from the beginning, and abode (stood) not in the truth, because there is no truth in him. When he speaketh a lie, he speaketh of his own:* **for he is a liar, and the father of it."** *John 8:44*

> *"And the great dragon was cast out, that old serpent, called the Devil, and*

> *Satan, which **deceiveth** the whole world."*   *Revelation 12:9*

Satan has always been big on flowery promises, but in the end, the same burning flames await him and all those who choose to follow his wicked path.

Teenager, please! Do *not* be deceived!

There's only one reason Satan wants you to serve him. He wants to get demons inside you so he can use you in his sicko plans, then eventually kill you, leaving you to pay the price forever.

Stop believing the devil's lies. He has nothing good to offer you. Don't be stupid. Look beyond his phony promises and see what Satan worship is really like.

* *If the thought of gulping down urine and blood doesn't appeal to you, stay away from the occult.*

* *If kicking a decapitated head around is not your idea of fun, steer clear of Satan.*

* *If eating a person's heart is not an ideal snack to you, avoid Satanism like the plague.*

* *If you do not want to fry in hell forever, you guessed it . . .*

Chapter 14

The Stairway's Last Step

You are almost there!

You have reached the last step on the stairway to hell.

The devil is through using you. Now it's time to toss you into the fiery flames.

You are about to experience horrors you never dreamed possible. Your shocked eyes will see dancing yellow flames and thick black smoke billowing upward. The stomach-turning stench of burning flesh will make you want to throw up.

Echoing in your ears will be the throat-shredding screams of millions who are scorching in the sizzling flames.

And there's no escape . . . *ever!*

Now you are about to be heaved into the fiery flames of hell. Like all those already there, you will scream in agony. You will beg to die, just to stop the pain. But you will never die . . . and the pain will never stop.

You believed the devil's lies, now it's time to pay. The most horrible place in the universe is about to become your eternal home. Welcome to hell.

> *"Now I can see it all clearly," you cry out.*
> *"The rock stars lied to me. They deceived me. I was so stupid. I wish I had listened. I should never . . . "*

But it's too late! Forever and ever, you will scream agonizing, blood-curdling screams. It won't matter that your rock gods are frying right next to you.

You Were Warned!

The worst part is, God tried to warn you. He didn't want you to end up here. All you had to do was pick up a Bible. God told you where you were headed:

> *"The wicked shall be turned into hell."*
> *Psalm 9.17*

God even described hell in great detail to warn you about how horrible it is. Here are just a few scriptures where God described this eternal prison of fire:

> *"And whosoever was not found written in the book of life was cast into the lake of fire."* Revelation 20:15

> *"Then shall he (God) say also unto them*

139

on the left hand, Depart from me, ye cursed, into everlasting fire, prepared for the devil and his angels." Matthew 25:41

*"And these shall go away into **everlasting** punishment . . . " Matthew 25:46*

You shouldn't have listened to that minister or evangelist who said there was no such place as hell. He was wrong! You should have listened to God's Word:

*"In flaming fire taking vengeance on them that know not God, and that obey not the gospel of our Lord Jesus Christ: Who shall be punished with **everlasting destruction."** II Thessalonians 1:8-9*

"But the fearful, and unbelieving, and the abominable, and murderers, and whoremongers, and sorcerers, and idolaters, and all liars, shall have their part in the lake which burneth with fire and brimstone." Revelation 21:8

"If any man worship the beast and his image . . . The same shall drink of the wine of the wrath of God . . . and he shall be tormented with fire and brimstone in the presence of the holy angels, and in the presence of the Lamb (Jesus): And the smoke of their torment ascendeth up forever and ever: and they have no rest day nor night . . . " Revelation 14:9-11

You shouldn't have listened to liars like Bon Scott, who said, "Hell Ain't A Bad Place To Be." He was wrong:

> *"But the children of the kingdom shall be cast into outer darkness: there shall be weeping and gnashing (grinding) of teeth."*   *Matthew 8:12*

> *" . . . to whom is reserved the blackness of darkness for ever."*   *Jude 13*

> *"Ye serpents, ye generation of vipers, how can ye escape the damnation of hell?"*   *Matthew 23:33*

Before you decide to follow Satan, you should know where he's leading you. He knows where he's headed. Now he wants you to be his eternal guest.

> *"And the devil that deceived them was cast into the lake of fire and brimstone, where the beast and the false prophet are, and shall be tormented day and night for ever and ever."*
> *Revelation 20:10*

The devil will spend eternity paying for his rebellion against God in a lake of fire and brimstone. Now you are about to join him there.

When you lie in bed at night, close your eyes and think about it:

> *"If my heart stops beating tonight, I will burn forever. I am on a ledge overlooking hell and the devil is quickly sneaking up behind me. He's about to shove me from behind into the red-hot flames."*

As you read these words, I know your enemy is screaming out to you:

> *"Don't believe what you are reading. It's not true. He doesn't know what he's talking about."*

The devil does not want you to know the truth. He doesn't want you to think about your destination for a split second. He's afraid he might lose you.

But it is true. You have believed the devil's dirty lies. You have followed his carefully laid stairway. You have taken the path to hell. Now you are almost there. It's time to burn.

Can you hear the screams in the distance? It's getting closer. Can you smell the sizzling flesh? Is the smoke burning your eyes yet?

"Don't believe what you're reading," the devil cries out in desperation. Now Satan is really starting to sweat. He's had you for so long. You are so close to hell. He doesn't want to lose you now.

But he's got a major problem. You just caught on to him. Now you know he's deceived you. You know you're headed for hell. Now you know Satan is your real enemy.

"Oh, no," the devil screams. More bad news. Now you're about to turn the page and find out that you can get off the stairway to hell right now and escape the eternal torment that's just ahead.

Satan calls an emergency meeting with his most powerful demons.

> *"We've got to stop this young person,"*
> *he orders. "Another teen is about to slip*
> *through our fingers. Somebody do some-*
> *thing . . . quick!"*

Satan knows you are about to hear the one message he hates more than any other . . .

Chapter 15

Your Only Hope

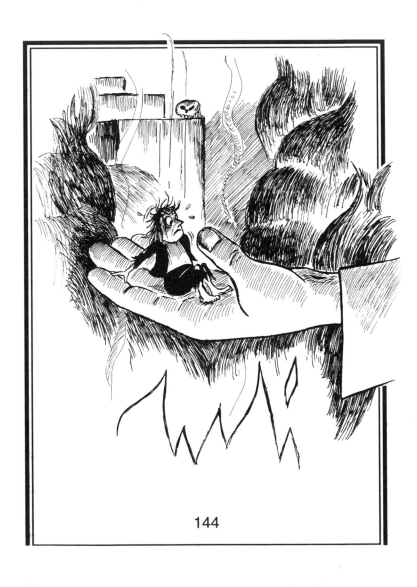

For teens who have already taken that last step down the stairway to hell, it is too late. There is no hope!

They were deceived by the devil, and their lives and souls have been destroyed. They will burn forever in the lake of fire . . .

And they will *never* get out!

But here comes the most exciting news you will ever hear. For you, there is hope! There is an answer!

Teenager, no matter what kind of problems you have right now, no matter how far down the devil's stairway you've fallen, there is an answer.

I have seen young people with every kind of problem we've talked about find the one and only answer and have their lives miraculously changed.

The first thing you must do is realize that you are in the middle of a spiritual war . . . a war for your soul.

The problems you are having are not accidental, they have been carefully planned by Satan.

> *"Be sober, be vigilant; because your adversary (enemy) the devil, as a roaring lion, walketh about, seeking whom he may devour:"*   *I Peter 5:8*

The devil is working overtime to destroy your life and your soul, but God has already done everything necessary to rescue you. God has provided the answer to your problems. What is that answer?

Jesus Christ!

Teenager, Jesus loves you! He loves you so much that He came to earth, suffered the agonizing pain of a cruel wooden cross and died one of the most painful deaths a human being can die. He was crucified.

His death on the cross paid the penalty for your sins and mine. Because Jesus died, you can have victory over the evil one.

Jesus Christ is the only One who can pull you off the stairway to hell and place your trembling feet on the rock-solid stairway to heaven. And the most exciting news is, He wants to do it for you. He wants to do it right now. It's up to you. The Bible says:

> *"The Lord is not . . . willing that any should perish, but that all should come to repentance."*   *II Peter 3:9*

Whether you know it or not, everyone (including you) serves somebody. Either you serve God or you serve the devil. You may say, "Not me, I don't serve either one." Wrong! God already settled that question:

> *"Know ye not, that to whom ye yield yourselves servants to obey, his servants ye are to whom ye obey; whether of sin unto death, or of obedience unto right-eousness."* Romans 6:16

Either you are serving God or you are serving Satan. When you willingly yield yourself to sin, you are a servant of Satan. Hopefully, you are saying by now:

> *"I want nothing more to do with Satan. How can I get off the stairway to hell?"*

There is only one way . . . and it's the most beautiful story in the whole world.

Real Love

Despite the fact that you have rebelled against God and spit in His face, God still loves you and wants to give you the most priceless gift in the world, the gift of eternal life in heaven. The Bible says that:

> *" . . . the gift of God is eternal life through Jesus Christ our Lord."* Romans 6:23

This very minute, you can escape from the dark and dreary stairway to hell and receive this beautiful gift

147

of eternal life. Here's what you must do:

First you must understand that you cannot earn eternal life. It is a gift:

> *"For by grace are ye saved through faith; and that not of yourselves: **it is the gift of God**: not of works, lest any man should boast."* Ephesians 2:8-9

No one deserves heaven because no one is without sin:

> *"As it is written, There is none righteous, no, not one:"* Romans 3:10

But God loved you so much that He sent His own Son, Jesus Christ, to shed His blood and die on the cross for you. Jesus never sinned, so He did not have to die. When He gave His life, He died for you:

> *"But God commendeth (proved) his love toward us, in that, while we were yet sinners, Christ died for us."* Romans 5:8

When Christ died, He shed pure and sinless blood to pay the price for your sins. Only the blood of Christ can wash away your sins:

> *" . . . the blood of Jesus Christ his (God's) Son cleanseth us from all sin."* I John 1:7

How can you get this gift of eternal life?

1. Repent – "turn away" from your sinful lifestyles. You can't live on the stairway to hell and go to heaven.

> "... except ye repent, ye shall all likewise perish." Luke 13:5

2. Accept Jesus Christ as the Lord and Master of your life. God's Word says:

> "That if thou shalt confess with thy mouth the Lord Jesus, and shalt believe in thine heart that God hath raised him from the dead, thou shalt be saved. For with the heart man believeth unto righteousness; and with the mouth confession is made unto salvation." Romans 10:9-10

The Bible promises that if you will call out to God with a sincere heart and ask Him to come into your heart and save you, He will:

> "For whosoever shall call upon the name of the Lord shall be saved." Romans 10:13

If you would like to escape Satan's evil clutches right now and accept Jesus Christ as your Lord and Savior, pray a sincere prayer from your heart like this:

Dear Lord Jesus,

> I'm so sorry for the life I've lived. I want to get off the stairway to hell and break

*the heavy chains that Satan has
wrapped around me. Please come into
my heart and save me. Please forgive
me of all my sins. I accept you right now
as my personal Lord, Master and Savior.
In Jesus' name I pray, Amen.*

If you just prayed that prayer and meant it, you are
now a child of God and have eternal life. You were
just snatched off the stairway to hell and are on your
way to the gold-paved streets of heaven:

*"But as many as received him, to them
gave he power to become the sons of
God, even to them that believe on his
name:"*   *John 1:12*

*"For God so loved the world, that he
gave his only begotten Son, that whoso-
ever believeth in him should not perish,
but have everlasting life."*   *John 3:16*

Young person, there is no other answer. Jesus Christ
is the **only** way. The Bible says in Acts 4:12:

*"Neither is there salvation in any other:
for there is none other name under
heaven given among men, whereby we
must be saved."*

I've worked with young people who have searched far
and wide for answers. They always came up empty
until they came to Jesus.

Many of their parents searched too. They tried psychiatrists, psychologists, therapists, counsellors, and so on. None of these "experts" could help their children because Jesus is the only answer. What the world and all its wisdom can never do, Jesus can do in an instant.

I wish I could share with you all the thrilling stories of changed lives I've seen over the years. There is nothing as exciting as watching Jesus Christ change a life. Here are just two examples.

Pam

Pam was physically and sexually abused as a child. She was dabbling in drugs and alcohol by six or seven. From there her life became a living nightmare. Full blown drug addiction and alcoholism followed.

She hated herself, hated life, and tried to commit suicide on several occasions. She was locked up and abused in mental institutions more than once. Her life was a cesspool of sex, including rape, lesbianism, sadomasochism and sex with animals.

She saw counsellors, therapists and others, yet no one could help her. Many experts told her she could not be helped. They said she was too far gone.

The Answer At Last

Finally, in desperation, she turned to Jesus Christ. She bowed her head and, with tears flowing down her face, she asked Jesus Christ to forgive her and come into her heart and save her.

The miracles started immediately. Her whole life began to change. Her frown turned into a smile. Her despair became joy. Her turmoil was replaced with a beautiful inner peace.

A young lady who once desperately wanted to die suddenly had an overwhelming zest for life.

Pam finally realized that Jesus Christ was her best friend. He loved her enough to willingly die on Calvary's cross so she could escape from the stairway to hell and enjoy real peace in this life and the glory and beauty of heaven forever. What a miracle!

George

In chapter 8, we talked about a young man named George, who had almost reached the last step of the stairway to hell. His life was wrecked. He was a drug addict, a drug dealer, a thief, a worthless bum by the world's standards.

He could have taken that last fatal step into the flames at any second. He was that close.

But in the nick of time, one cold and lonely night he bowed his head and asked God to forgive him of all his sins. He asked Jesus Christ to come into his heart and save him. He repented of his sins and promised God he would change his lifestyle.

At that moment, George became a child of God. His name was written in the Lamb's Book of Life and God's strong hand lifted him off the stairway to hell. Angels in heaven rejoiced. Jesus rejoiced. It was the greatest moment of George's life.

From that moment on, George's life was never the same. With God's help, he quit taking and dealing drugs, and stopped drinking. His whole life became new. George was living proof that this verse is true:

> *"Therefore if any man be in Christ, he is a new creature (creation): old things are passed away; behold, all things are become new."*   *II Corinthians 5:17*

For years, George had wanted to clean up his life, but he never could. Instead, he always fell deeper into the muck. But when he asked Jesus to come into his heart, Jesus did what George could never do.

For the first time in his life, George was really happy. His anger, hate and rebellion were replaced with a beautiful peace that cannot be described.

You say, "It can't be that simple." It wasn't simple for Jesus. It cost the Lord His life. But He willingly paid the price for our sins, a price we could never pay.

God Will Change Anyone

I saw the same beautiful change take place in hundreds of other teens. The types of young people God has cured is endless; drug addicts, prostitutes, abuse victims, alcoholics, runaways and throwaways. They've all found that Jesus is the only answer.

Teenager, the same Jesus who reached down in love and saved each of those teens wants to do the same for you, if you will invite Him into your heart and turn away from your sinful life.

Don't say, "I can't change," until you see what can happen with Jesus living in your heart. God can do anything, if you will let Him.

> *"But Jesus . . . said unto them, With men this is impossible; but with God all things are possible."*   *Matthew 19:26*

As you finish this chapter, you have made a choice. You decided one of two things. You said either:

> *"Yes! I want Jesus Christ to come into my heart so I can enjoy the peace of being a child of God and the assurance of eternal life in heaven."*

Or you uttered a resounding:

> *"No! I want nothing to do with Jesus Christ. I'd rather live on the stairway to hell, and burn in the lake of fire than have Christ in my life."*

I pray you made the right decision.

TEENAGER: GOD MEETS EVERY NEED

God is the real thing, like Coca-Cola
He works wonders, like Bayer Aspirin
He brings good things to life, like G. E.
He gets the stain out, like Tide
He makes you feel great, like Frosted Flakes
He puts us in good hands, like Allstate
He's pure, like Ivory soap
He cares enough to send the best, like Hallmark
He sounds better the more you hear Him, like
     AT & T
He gives 100% relief, like Rolaids
He makes us glad to know Him, like Dial soap
He's a neighbor who's always there, like
     State Farm
He's good til the last drop, like Maxwell House
He covers the earth, like Sherwin Williams
He speaks, and people listen, like E.F. Hutton
He treats you right, like Dairy Queen
He's there to hear you, like Bell-Tone
He's here today and here tomorrow, like
     Frigidaire;
He's the right choice, like AT & T

Chapter 16

Five Steps
In The Right Direction

If you are now a true Christian, your whole life will begin to change, not because you have to, but because you want to.

Remember, in the last chapter we said that to be a true Christian you must be willing to repent, or turn away from your sinful lifestyle.

> *"Having therefore these promises, dearly beloved, let us cleanse ourselves from all filthiness of the flesh and spirit, perfecting holiness in the fear of God."*
> *II Corinthians 7:1*

When people truly understand what Jesus Christ did for them on the cross, they will do anything they can to please the One who saved them.

If you sat in a cell on death row and were scheduled to be executed the next morning, and your best friend came and died in the electric chair for you the night before, you would love that person beyond words.

Teen, that's what Jesus did for you. He saw you barreling head-long down the stairway to hell and knew that if He didn't die in your place, you would burn forever in hell.

So He came to earth, lived 33 years as a man, then gave His life on the cross, so you and I could go free.

When young people (or adults) say things like, "I don't care what God wants, I want what I want," you can be sure they know nothing about real salvation and have no appreciation for what Christ did for them on the cross.

If you are truly saved, you don't "have to change," you "want to change." You long to do anything you can to please the One who gave His life for you and purchased your eternal salvation.

Here are a few changes you need to make right away. Each one will help you start pleasing your new Master and turning your back on your old one:

Clean House

Get rid of any items you own that are dedicated to Satan. This includes rock albums, tapes or C. D.'s. Anything else associated with rock music should also go, including posters, T-shirts, magazines, etc.

Also included on the "get rid of" list should be D & D materials, occult books, occult jewelry, pornography, ouija boards and anything else that was created for

Satan's use. The Bible says the best way to get rid of these Satanic tools is to burn them:

> *"The graven images of their gods (idols) shall ye **burn with fire . . . "***
> *Deuteronomy 7:25*

> *"Many of them also which used curious (magic) arts brought their books together, and **burned them** before all men:"*
> *Acts 19:19*

It is crucial that you clean out your room and your house. Satan and his demons can use anything you keep to destroy you.

> *"Neither shalt thou bring an abomination into thine house, **lest thou be a cursed thing like it**: but thou shalt utterly detest it, and thou shalt utterly abhor (hate) it; for it is a cursed thing."*
> *Deuteronomy 7:26*

When you play with Satan's toys, you are flirting with real demons. To cut those ties once and for all, burn everything you have that is from the devil.

Read God's Word

While you were traveling down the stairway to hell, Satan was pumping his trashy lies into you like gas into an empty car. T.V., movies, music, videos, magazines, the list is endless.

Now that you know Jesus Christ, you need to start learning the truth. For that, you must read and study your Bible every day.

> *"Sanctify (make them holy) through thy truth: thy word is truth."*   John 17:17

Reading the Bible every day will do many things for you. It will show you how to escape from the satanic sinful lifestyle that used to enslave you:

> *"Wherewithal shall a young man cleanse his way? by taking heed thereto according to thy word."*   Psalm 119:9

> *"Thy word have I hid in mine heart, that I might not sin against thee."*
> Psalm 119:11

The Bible is God's love letter to you. When you read your Bible, that is how God talks to you. Read it every day to find out how much God really loves you.

Talk To God

The difference between true Christianity and religion is very simple. Religion is man seeking God. Christianity is developing a personal relationship with God once you have found Him.

God loves you and wants to be your friend. He wants you to talk to Him in prayer. The Bible tells us to:

"Pray without ceasing."
I Thessalonians 5:17

"The sacrifice of the wicked is an abomi-
nation to the Lord: but the prayer of the
upright is his delight."   *Proverbs 15:8*

When your burdens and cares are crushing you, pour out your heart to God.   He's waiting to hear and answer your prayers. A famous song called, What A Friend, says this about prayer:

What a Friend we have in Jesus,
All our sins and griefs to bear!
What a privilege to carry
Everything to God in prayer!

O what peace we often forfeit,
O what needless pain we bear,
All because we do not carry
Everything to God in prayer!

When you pray, it doesn't have to be a stiff, formal ceremony. Just talk to God like you would talk to your best friend. God hates long-winded gas-bag prayers. God wants to throw up when He hears the prayers of religious phonies who try to impress people with their pious ramblings.

New Friends

If you crawl in a sewer you will come out stinking. In the same way, if you hang with teens who are into drugs, crime, sex and Satan worship, you will never please God yourself.

You should start praying immediately that God will bring other genuine Christians into your life that you can become friends with.

This is where your Christianity will really be put to the test. Who is more important to you, Jesus Christ or your old friends? If your Christianity is genuine, you will want to spend time with people who love God and enjoy talking about spiritual things.

One of your toughest jobs will be telling your old friends that you have changed, that you no longer do the things you used to do.

Expect to be laughed at and made fun of. It hurts, but there is no way around it. To begin growing as a Christian, you will have to stop surrounding yourself with servants of Satan.

A New Best Friend

You can take great comfort, though, knowing you have a new best friend. God not only created the universe and holds it all together, he also loves you and wants to be your best friend. The Bible says God is a friend:

> "... that sticketh closer than a brother."
> Proverbs 18:24

God Will Change You

As you read God's Word, you will begin feeling guilty about certain areas in your life. When that happens, change those areas and do what the Bible says.

The Holy Spirit will teach you everything you need to know as a Christian and will guide you into all truth. (See John 16:13.)

There are many areas in your life that you will need to change, but don't get discouraged. God loves you and can work miracles in your life that you never thought possible. I've seen him do it for hundreds of other teens. He can do it for you too!

In the past, Satan was able to get you to rebel against God. Now you need to learn to obey God. Do what His Word says. The more you obey, the more God will bless you and the happier you will be.

Keep your eyes on Christ. Don't worry about what others do in the name of Christianity. Men will always fail you, but Jesus Christ will never let you down.

Chapter 17

Don't Get Fooled Again

Before you met Christ, Satan had you fooled.

Now that you are a genuine Christian, don't let him fool you again.

I guarantee you . . . *he will try*!

Around the world, millions of deceived church-going people think they are serving and pleasing God, when they are really sliding down the same stairway to hell you just got off.

You need to understand that the devil is working just as hard in Bible preaching churches as he is inside rock concert arenas.

He has just as many of his people in key positions in Christian churches and ministries as he has in Heavy Metal rock bands.

Christianity today is a total mess. Our world is crawl-ing with false Christians, false churches, false teachers and preachers, and false doctrines. It is up to you to sort out the phony from the genuine.

This chapter will help make sure you don't get fooled again. In it we will expose some of the false teachings and practices that are deceiving millions today, all in the name of Christianity.

False Christians

Almost everyone now claims to be a born again Christian. Polls indicate that 55% of all Americans say they are saved. But the Bible says it isn't so:

> *"Enter ye in at the strait gate: for wide is the gate, and broad is the way, that leadeth to destruction, and **many** there be which go in thereat: Because straight is the gate, and narrow is the way, which leadeth unto life, and **few** there be that find it."*   *Matthew 7:13-14*

If a person talks like the world, lives like the world, looks like the world, chances are he is of the world. Just because someone says he is a Christian means nothing. His life must show it.

False Churches

Churches today can range from social clubs to fronts for Satanic covens. To help you know the good from the bad, ask yourself these questions about any church you go to:

1. Are the church services based on feelings or facts? Are they a time of real spiritual feeding or emotional hype? Hype you can get at a rock concert or a carnival. The job of the pastor is to feed and strengthen his sheep.

2. Has the church been infiltrated by Satanists? The Bible says that true Bible believing churches will be infiltrated.

> *"For such are false apostles, deceitful workers, transforming themselves into the apostles of Christ. And no marvel; for Satan himself is transformed into an angel of light. Therefore it is no great thing if his ministers also be transformed as the ministers of righteousness . . . "*
> *II Corinthians 11:13-15*

If you are in a church where people are being converted to Christ and lives are changing, chances are Satanist infiltrators are there. Watch out!

3. Are people being genuinely saved? Are their lives changing after salvation?

4. Are church members growing spiritually, or do they act just like people out in the world?

5. Is sin condemned or condoned? Many pastors are scared to death to preach the truth to their people because they might lose them. If a pastor won't cry out against sin, the church is not worth your time.

6. Are church members opening themselves up for a demonic attack? The Bible instructs us to:

> *"Lay hands suddenly on no man, neither be partaker of other men's sins: keep thyself pure."* I Timothy 5:22

The practice of "laying on of hands" in widely used in many churches. It is also one of the Satanists' favorite means of transferring demons. Be very careful before you let anyone lay hands on you.

False Teachers And Preachers

Just because a man gets up and says, "Thus saith the Lord," does not mean he is a servant of God:

> *"For thus saith the Lord of hosts, the God of Israel; Let not your prophets and your diviners, that be in the midst of you, deceive you, neither hearken to your dreams which ye cause to be dreamed.* **For they prophesy falsely unto you in my name: I have not sent them, saith the Lord."** Jeremiah 29:8-9

God says it is your responsibility not to let these false prophets deceive you. You must be on the lookout.

> *"Then the Lord said unto me, The prophets prophesy lies in my name: I sent them not, neither have I commanded them, neither spake unto them: they*

prophesy unto you a false vision and divination, and a thing of nought, and the deceit of their heart."   Jeremiah 14:14

As the times get worse, so will these false preachers:

"But evil men and seducers (imposters) shall wax worse and worse, deceiving and being deceived."   II Timothy 3:13

Strong's Concordance defines those imposters as "a wizard (as muttering spells)."[1]

God here reveals to us that Satan will plant his imposters in churches. Their job is to destroy every true Christian they can . . . **from the inside**.

False Music

Now that Christ lives in your heart, one of your first steps should be to burn all your secular rock music. But before you race out to the local Christian bookstore to replace it with Christian music, there is something you need to know.

Much of the modern music that wears the name "Christian" is **not** Christian at all. Jeff Godwin's excellent book **Dancing With Demons, The Music's Real Master** exposes Satan in a variety of today's "Christian" music, including everything from Contemporary Christian to "Christian" Heavy Metal.

Before you buy your first Christian album, get Jeff's

book, available from Chick Publications. For now, here are a few questions you need to ask about any "Christian" music you listen to:

1. *Who receives the real praise from their music, Jesus Christ or the "performer?"*

2. *Are you more interested in the music or the message?*

3. *Does the music soothe your heart or make your flesh crawl?*

4. *Is there any spiritual depth to the lyrics of the songs? Much of today's so-called "Christian" stuff can't have much of a spiritual message because it hardly even mentions God.*

True Christian music will bring honor and glory to Jesus Christ, not to the performer. The message will be more important than the music and it will soothe your heart. As you will learn, real Christian music is very rare these days.

Be On Guard

Satan will not give up on you just because you are now a Christian. Though he can never destroy your soul, he will do everything he can to shatter your walk with God and destroy your testimony before others.

The devil is furious that he lost you. He had you in

his grasp, but you slipped away. So you won't get fooled again, God commands you to study your Bible:

> *"Study to shew thyself approved unto God, a workman that needeth not to be ashamed, rightly dividing the word of truth."* II Timothy 2:15

Don't worry about what men are saying. Find out what you believe from God's Word. In these evil last days, false teachings are running wild. Deceivers are leading millions astray. Studying God's Word will ground you so the following verse won't describe you:

> *"That we henceforth be no more children, tossed to and fro, and carried about with every wind of doctrine, by the sleight of men, and cunning craftiness, whereby they lie in wait to deceive;"*
> *Ephesians 4:14*

To better understand basic Bible doctrines, you should get the book, **The Next Step**, published by Chick Publications.

In a word, teen, be on guard. There are false churches and infiltrated churches out there. False teachers, preachers and evangelists are filling pulpits everywhere. Most so-called Christian music is totally heathen. Beware! The fact that it wears the name "Christian" means nothing anymore.

The devil fooled you once. Don't let him do it again.

Chapter 18

For Teens Who Have No One

Teen, if you are all alone in this world and no one cares about you, this chapter is for you.

Though most people have no idea how rotten life is for you, I have a very special message that will help you:

* *If a subway tunnel or a park bench is your home, and you pick your meals out of gar-bage cans, I'm talking to you right now.*

* *If you are a throwaway, living on your own, this message is for you.*

* *If you wear the bruises and scars of physical abuse, this is for you.*

* *If your parents are dead or have taken off, keep reading.*

* *If you endure the nightmare of incest and have no one to turn to, this chapter is for you.*

No matter how terrible your life has been, no matter how much pain and suffering you have endured, there is one exciting message I'm glad I can tell you:

Jesus . . . loves . . . *you!*

I can't tell you why you've had such a horrible life so far, but I can tell you that Jesus loves you.

I know you didn't ask to be an incest victim and it doesn't seem fair. I don't know why you have been forced to live through that kind of hell, but I do know that Jesus loves you.

You didn't ask your parents to divorce, or die, or disappear, and leave you on your own. I know your heart aches every day. I don't know why it happened, but I do know that Jesus loves you.

I know you think about suicide a lot, but I must tell you before you end it all . . . Jesus loves *you!*

Thousands of teens are labeled "bad kids." But many of those "bad kids" aren't bad at all, they've just never had a chance. Life dealt them a rotten hand.

Never Had A Chance

Ruben's mom was a prostitute. His dad was a drug addict. Ruben remembers as a child opening the bathroom door and seeing his dad passed out on the floor with a needle stuck in his arm and puddles of blood on the floor.

Ruben wasn't a bad kid. He just needed someone to tell him that Jesus loved him and could help him.

I read about a heroin addict who gave birth to a son. Thanks to his mother's raging drug habit, this innocent little baby was addicted to drugs at birth. He was going through withdrawals as he was delivered.

Millions of young people around the world share this poor infant's problem. This precious baby didn't ask for life to be so cold and cruel, but it happened. For the rest of his life he will pay for his parent's sins. That is, unless he trusts Jesus Christ as his Savior.

The same goes for you. No matter how cruel life has been to you, I know one thing beyond any doubt . . . Jesus loves you and wants to help you.

As we talked about in chapter 15, Jesus loves you so much that He willingly gave His life so you could someday live with Him in heaven. He also wants to help you while you're still here on earth.

These beautiful and comforting words from the Bible tell us what we should do with our heavy burdens:

> *"Cast thy burden upon the Lord, and he shall sustain thee: he shall never suffer the righteous to be moved." Psalm 55:22*

> *"Casting all your care upon him (God); for he careth for you."*   *I Peter 5:7*

Lonely teen, God's heart breaks when he sees you hurting. He is loving, compassionate and kind. He is perfect love.

Despite your rotten circumstances, bow your head right now and accept Christ. He's waiting to do wonderful things for you.

> *"But thou, O Lord, art a God full of compassion, and gracious, longsuffering, and plenteous in mercy and truth."*
> *Psalm 86:15*

Jesus said:

> *"Come unto me, all ye that labour and are heavy laden, and I will give your rest. Take my yoke upon you, and learn of me; for I am meek and lowly in heart: and ye shall find rest unto your souls. For my yoke is easy and my burden is light."*
> *Matthew 11:28-30*

Don't get me wrong. Your horrors will not end overnight. You won't wake up tomorrow in some sort of fairyland. But you will be a child of God. And God takes good care of his children.

Trapped

The first time Melissa's father raped her, she was just a child. The abuse went on for years. She held all the pain inside because she was scared to talk about it with anyone. At first she hated her father. Then she hated herself. Her life was a never-ending nightmare. There was no escape and no light at the end of the tunnel.

One night, a tiny voice spoke to her heart and said, "If you will trust in Me, and put all your burdens and cares on My shoulders, I'll get you through this."

That night, Melissa accepted Jesus Christ as her personal Savior. Relief came instantly as Jesus lifted the heavy burdens off her shoulders. She no longer had to carry them alone.

Soon a faint ray of light cracked into her world of darkness. The light grew until it shone brightly. God answered this young girl's prayers. She was removed from her home and adopted by a fine Christian couple.

Today, the past is only a bad memory. Her life is totally changed. Her new parents love her and treat her like a princess. Joy now fills every day. Miraculously, Jesus took away the hate that once gripped her heart and replaced it with genuine love.

Why?

Why did she have to endure all that suffering? I don't know. Maybe it was so she could relate to hurting teens like you and feel compassion for you.

Maybe it was so you would listen when she told you that Jesus Christ is the *only* answer to your problems.

I don't know why, but I do know that God can do for you what He did for Melissa. It may look impossible, but it looked just as impossible for Melissa when she heard her father climbing the steps to her room whenever her mom left in the car.

The same God who performed the miracles in Melissa's life can do the "impossible" in your life too, if you will give Him your life.

Don't Get Mad At God

Young person, if you've had unfair breaks in life, you are a favorite target for Satan. He has a carefully planned stairway to hell all laid out for you. Here's how he deceives young people like you.

First he plants thoughts in your mind like:

> *"How could God let this happen to me?*
> *If God really loved me, He wouldn't make*
> *me go through all this."*

Gradually you get bitter against God and begin to hate Him. Satan bombards your mind with lies like:

* *It's all God's fault.*
* *He doesn't love you.*
* *Look at the way He's treating you.*
* *How could a God of love let this happen to you?*

If the devil can get you to blame God for your problems, he's got you. You see, if you stay mad at God, you will reject His Son, Jesus. When you reject Christ, you turn your back on the **only** One who can help you. And Satan knows it.

The devil just deceived you into making the worst mistake of your life; one that will cost you an eternity in hell. And if you think you are hurting now, wait 'till the scalding flames of hell engulf you.

All Satan cares about is that you never trust Christ and get plucked off the stairway to hell. If he can use your bad circumstances to reach his goal, he will.

Teen, God loves you. He wants to help you. He wants to change your life. He longs to see a smile on your face instead of a frown. And most importantly, He wants you to escape from the stairway to hell and live with Him in heaven forever.

Here's what you must do:

1. *Stop listening to the devil when he tells you to blame God for all your problems.*

2. *Realize that it's Satan who enjoys watching you suffer. It breaks God's heart to see you crying in agony.*

3. *Reject Satan's lies and ask Jesus Christ to come into your heart and save you.*

4. *Cast all your burdens and cares on the Lord.*

He loves you and wants to lift those heavy burdens off your shoulders.

5. *Ask God to perform miracles in your life, like He did for Melissa.*

Lonely teen, the nightmare can end right now. Jesus Christ is standing at the door of your heart, waiting for you to ask Him in so He can begin helping you.

How much does Jesus love you? The Bible says:

"Greater love hath no man than this, that a man lay down his life for his friends."
John 15:13

Jesus loved you so much that He died for you. There is no greater love than that. Don't blame Him for your problems. Fall on your face and repent. Ask Jesus to come into your heart and save you.

Learn to hate the devil. He's the one who smiles with delight when you are in misery. He's the one who wants to see you burn in hell.

Young person, if you think nobody cares about you, you're wrong. Jesus cares. He wants to be your best friend. He loves you. He wants to guide your path through this cold, heartless world.

Trust Christ as your Savior right now. Then ask Him to take care of those problems. He's waiting for you with his arms open wide. . .

Chapter 19

For "Christian" Teens Only

"I was born and raised in a preacher's home.

"I prayed the sinners prayer when I was six years old.

"I've been in Christian school all my life.

"I've never missed a youth meeting.

"I'm so glad I'm a Christian and I don't have to worry about going to hell."

John is one of the saddest cases of all. You see, at the age of 21 his car veered off a slippery road and slid over a cliff. He was killed instantly.

When it came time for him to stand before God, John proudly marched in, head held high. He could hardly wait to grab the keys to his brand new mansion and take his first tour down the gold-paved streets of heaven. After all, he was a Christian, wasn't he?

Finally it was John's turn. He trembled in shocked disbelief as he heard God say the following:

"I never knew you: depart from me."

John fired back:

"God, surely you can't be talking to me. I was a pastor's son. I prayed the sinners prayer when I was 6. I was a . . ."

God cut him off and continued:

"Depart from me, ye cursed, into everlasting fire, prepared for the devil and his angels."

Though he had played the Christianity game, John was sent to hell, where he will burn forever.

What a tragedy!

All his life, John was riding the stairway to hell . . . but he thought he was assured of heaven because he recited a little prayer as a child.

It wasn't until he died and it was too late that John learned the horrible truth . . . he too had been deceived by his enemy, Satan.

Millions More

The biggest tragedy is that there are millions more

just like John, who believe they can live like they want to and still go to heaven because one day they prayed a prayer and asked Jesus to come into their heart.

Though their lives were a total wreck, many of the troubled teens I worked with claimed to be born again Christians. One of our first jobs was to strip away Satan's mask of confusion and show them they were really headed straight for damnation in hell.

"Christian" teen, I've got a question for you. **Are you really a Christian?**

Before you toss at me the fact that you whistled off a quick salvation prayer when you were eight, let's look at some scriptures:

> *"Ye adulterers and adulteresses, know ye not that the friendship of the world is enmity (hatred) with God? whosoever therefore will be a friend of the world is the enemy of God."*   *James 4:4*

Did you catch that, teen? If you love the world, **you** are an enemy of God.

If I had to sum up the average church youth group from the hundreds I've seen, I would have to say, "they love the world." They look like the world, talk like the world, act like the world, think like the world and sin like the world.

How about you, "Christian" teen. Let's drop that

phony religious mask you wear and take a look at the real you. Who do you really love? God . . . or the world? Don't lie.

* *Which do you love more, Amazing Grace, or the devil's latest rock song? Be honest.*

* *Which would you rather do, read your Bible or smoke pot with your friends?*

* *Do you hate God's rules and wish you could be like your peers out in the world?*

Who do you love? God . . . or the world? If you love the world, God says you are His **enemy!**

How Can They Be Saved?

Tammy had just trusted Christ as her Savior. She was so excited about her new-found faith in Christ. Her drinking and smoking had ended. She burned all her rock music and confessed all her other sins.

She was bursting with joy. The peace and contentment of knowing Christ made her face glow. At last she saw it all clearly . . . Satan had deceived her. His teasers had kept her on the stairway to hell. But now Christ had set her free. She was looking forward to the next step, meeting other Christian teens she could fellowship with.

Sunday morning she dressed quickly and raced to church in time for the teen Sunday School class. She could hardly wait to make some godly friends at this Bible believing, Bible preaching, soul-winning church.

Her heart soon sank. She overheard the lust-filled conversation of two girls behind her. They were discussing the secular rock concert they were going to with their boyfriends. They were upset because they had to bring their own beer.

These fine upstanding church members were into all the same sins Christ had just set Tammy free from.

Tammy was shocked! These girls didn't love God, they loved the world! "How could they be Christians and faithfully serve Satan year after year after year," she wondered. Simple Tammy, they can't!

"Christian" teen, you may think you're fooling everybody with your pious front, but God sees right through it. If you think you can smoke pot, drink, have sex, listen to rock music, lie and steal, and still go to heaven because you prayed a prayer one day, make no mistake about it . . . you are dead wrong.

Like your lost friends, *you* are on the stairway to hell!

True Christians don't love the world, they love God. The Bible makes that very plain:

> *"Love not the world, neither the things that are in the world. If any man love the world, the love of the Father is not in him."* I John 2:15

"Christian" teen, check your salvation. If you love the things of the world more than the things of God, the Bible says you are God's enemy.

"I'm Already A Christian"

I remember the day Diane stomped into my office. She was 13 years old and her life had already been ripped to shreds by sin.

* *She had been sexually active for two years.*

* *She had spent the last eight months locked in a mental hospital for trying to stab her mother to death with a butcher knife.*

* *She was addicted to drugs and alcohol and couldn't function without prescribed drugs.*

* *She wanted nothing to do with God or any rules. Total rebellion ruled her life.*

During our conversation, she became highly upset when I told her that Jesus Christ was the only answer to her problems.

She boldly pronounced that she was already a born again Christian. She bragged about how she had prayed the sinners prayer at a Christian youth camp several years before. How deceived!

Tragically, she was not a rare case. Many of the young people I interviewed felt that regardless of their lifestyle, they were saved because they had muttered some words years ago.

Please don't misunderstand. You are saved by faith, not by works. Only the shed blood of Christ can wash away our sins.

> *"For by grace are ye saved through faith; and that not of yourselves: it is the gift of God: Not of works, lest any man should boast."*   *Ephesians 2:8-9*

But once you become genuinely saved, your life **will** change. You cannot accept Christ as your Lord and Master, then keep serving your old master, Satan.

> *"No man can serve two masters: for either he will hate the one, and love the other; or he will hold to the one, and despise the other . . ."*   *Matthew 6:24*

"I'm Already A Christian"

Joe is another young man who comes to mind. In utter desperation, his parents brought their hard-hearted son to us for help. His life was going down faster than a toilet being flushed. He had been arrested several times and his criminal convictions were piling up. His life revolved around drugs, alcohol, rock music and crime.

He refused to obey any rules. He would do only what he wanted. No one was going to tell him what to do.

Before he left, I told him he needed Christ as his Savior. To my shock, he announced, "I'm already a Christian." He too had spit out some words about asking Jesus to save him many years ago.

Joe was no more saved than the man in the moon. He had believed one of the devil's biggest lies. He thought he could mumble a few words about Christ saving him, then go on doing whatever he wanted, and still wind up in heaven.

Christian youth groups everywhere are overflowing with deceived young people who are in the same sinking boat.

"Christian" teen, maybe the reason you can't get any victory in your Christian life is because you aren't really a Christian. You may have recited a little prayer, but there's more to salvation than that:

* *Have you ever turned over control of your life to Jesus Christ and made Him your Lord and Master?*

* *Have you ever repented of your sinful life and vowed to change it?*

Don't deceive yourself, teen. Are you really saved?

Far and away, the biggest problem I've found with "Christian" teens is that they aren't Christians at all.

If the Holy Spirit is convicting you right now, swallow

your pride and settle the salvation issue once and for all. Repent of your sins. Turn your back on the devil and all his toys. Give your heart and life to Jesus Christ, and get off Satan's stairway to hell.

You'll be amazed at the change in your life once you are genuinely saved.

Chapter 20

Just For Mom and Dad

Mom and dad, for nineteen chapters the gun barrel of this book has been pointed right at your teenager.

Now I must direct one chapter at you.

After interviewing hundreds of sets of parents and hundreds of single parents, I must admit that much of the blame for the way kids turn out must be laid squarely at the feet of the parents.

Before your son or daughter tries to use this chapter as a cop-out for their rebellious ways, let me say this. By the time a child reaches their teenage years, they are responsible for their own actions. The "it's not my fault the way I turned out; it's my parents fault" philosophy won't cut the mustard.

The Bible cuts that cop-out short with this verse:

> *"So then every one of us shall give account of **himself** to God." Romans 14:12*

We all will answer for our own lives. We won't be able to blame our sins on anyone else.

So this chapter is not meant to be a tool kids can use on their parents. It is included only to help moms and dads better understand how the enemy will use them to help destroy their own children.

I vividly remember one interview in particular. A set of parents had brought their teenage daughter because she kept running away. After about fifteen minutes of listening to her mother ramble on non-stop, I knew how the poor girl felt. I felt like running away too. Fortunately, I was able to control myself and remain in my office.

Listed below are eight important principles for raising a teenager. After working with thousands of teens, I believe these are the eight most important principles to help keep your teenager off the stairway to hell.

1. Example.

You must be what you want your kids to be. The "do as I say, not as I do" philosophy will never work. Your kids will "do as you do" every single time.

* A desperate father told me once that he had tried everything to get his son to quit smoking. Everything, that is, except quit smoking himself.

* Alcoholic fathers have asked me why they

couldn't stop their children from drinking.

* *Mothers who were having sex with men who were not their husband have told me they couldn't figure out why their young teenage daughters were sexually active.*

* *Parents who have spit in God's face and rebelled against Him for years have been unable to understand why the hearts of their teenage children are hardened towards God.*

You see, if it's not important enough for mom and dad to do, young people assume it's not important enough for them to do. Before you as a parent do anything, ask yourself: "How would I feel if my son or daughter did this?" Successful parents rearrange their lives to provide a good example for their children.

After years of instructions, lectures and countless talks, your children will follow your example. Make sure it's a good one.

2. Consistency.

One of the most important principles young people need to understand is the difference between right and wrong. We live in a society with no absolutes, no black and white, only many different shades of gray. Teenagers desperately need to learn that there are many absolute rights and many absolute wrongs.

To teach this essential principle, parents must be consistent in their discipline, their teaching and their example. If something is wrong today, it better be wrong tomorrow. If it was O.K. for the last three months, it better be O.K. today.

Inconsistency breeds confusion and lack of respect. Establish your rules, then be consistent. There is a tremendous amount of security in young people who have an established set of rules to live by.

A young person listens to rock music every day. Then, one day you bust down his door and take a sledge hammer to his rock records. Your teen is left wondering, "Is rock music bad? If so, why wasn't it bad before?"

A thousand other possible reasons for the outburst may race through his confused mind. "Is dad mad at me?" "Was I playing the music too loud?" "Is dad in a bad mood and taking it out on me?"

Whatever conclusions he finally comes to, you can be sure of one thing. He will grow increasingly confused and have less respect for you.

3. **Communication.**

Talk with your children. Learn how to communicate with them. One of Satan's most powerful tools in the destruction of young people is that he breaks off all meaningful communication between parents and their teenage children.

Get to know how your teen feels, where he's going, who he's hanging with and what they're doing. Talk with him about his problems, goals, friends, etc.

Openly admit to him your feelings, your frustrations and your desires for his well being. But you must be honest, sincere and genuine. Kids can spot an act ten miles away.

4. Spiritual training.

Without proper spiritual training, your child has **no** hope. Jesus said, "Ye must be born again" (John 3:7). Without Jesus Christ in his life, your child loses all the way around:

* *After he dies, he is doomed to an eternity in hell.*

* *While he is still alive, he is wide open to Satan's life-destroying attacks. Only Jesus Christ can safely guide teenagers through the treacherous paths they must walk today.*

As a parent, your most important responsibility is to provide your children with proper spiritual training. God gives this solemn warning to parents in Deuteronomy 6:6-7:

> *"And these words (the Bible), which I command thee this day, shall be in thine heart: **And thou shalt teach them dili-***

gently unto thy children, and shalt talk of them when thou sittest in thine house, and when thou walketh by the way, and when thou liest down, and when thou risest up."

Unless you as a parent know Jesus Christ personally and He resides in your heart, you will never be able to provide your children with proper spiritual training. If you do not know Christ as your Savior, go back and read chapter 15.

5. Love.

Your love for your children must be real. It must show up both in your words and in your actions. Teenagers can tell very easily when you are just saying something you really don't mean. You need to tell them often that you really love them, but it must go far beyond that.

You must also love them enough to alter your life for their good. You must be willing to discipline them, pray and fast for them (see Mark 9:29) and be willing to spend quality time with them by giving them your undivided attention. You must be willing to let them get mad at you when they don't understand that you are doing something for their good.

I remember a young lady who was not doing too well at the home where I worked. One day her aunt and uncle called to see if they could take her on an all-expense-paid vacation trip to Disney World in Florida.

I knew that if she left for two weeks, she would never come back and would return to the streets and her former troubles. When she found out that I said she couldn't go, she was not real happy, to say the least.

I explained to her that if she wanted to be mad at me, that was fine. I told her that I loved her enough to be willing to have her hate me if it meant helping save her life from destruction. When she finally understood why I had squashed her trip, she appreciated someone taking that kind of stand to help her.

Love your kids enough to make them do things they don't want to do. Successful adults spend most of their time doing things they don't want to do. Teenagers who never learn this character trait are doomed to failure. You're not helping them by letting them off, you're killing them.

6. Discipline.

Fair and consistent Biblical discipline is essential. Without it, your kids don't have a chance. Ninety-nine percent of the troubled young people I worked with had almost no discipline in the home. Lack of discipline always leads to ruin.

In millions of homes around the world, parents need to rise up and take control of their home back from their children. If children are to turn out right, parents *must* rule the home. I was always sickened when I heard parents say things like, "If he doesn't want to, what am I supposed to do?"

I remember a Mom and Dad who told me their 14-year-old son blasted rock music on his stereo while locked in his room in the basement. They hated it and knew it was wrong, but said there was nothing they could do about it because he kept his door locked.

They were both totally shocked when I suggested that they get a sledge hammer, smash the door down, then take the hammer to his stereo and records.

Parents, stop letting your kids run your home. Rise up and take the leadership position God commands you take. The Bible says that if you will not discipline your children, then you don't really love them, you hate them:

> *"He that spareth his rod hateth his son: but he that loveth him chasteneth (disciplines) him betimes (early).*
> *Proverbs 13:24*

7. Work.

Teach your children to work at a young age. Breed it into them. Lazy children grow up to become lazy adults and lazy adults are failures, no matter what else they have going for them.

Many of the teens I worked with were among the laziest creatures God ever created. Getting them to work was like trying to get a stubborn mule to move. I will never forget the pitiful 16-year-old healthy teen-age boy who wrote home to his mother after he was

199

made to work for almost three hours one day. His letter went something like this:

"Dear Mom,

Please get me out of here. It's awful. I hate it. I can't stand it here. They made me work all the way from nine in the morning 'til lunch time."

I asked him if he had ever worked one full day in his 16 years on God's green earth. To my shock, he said no. He left shortly after that. He liked it better lying around his parents house, sleeping all day and partying all night.

8. Honesty.

If you are to be successful as a parent, one thing you must have from your children is their respect. They will never follow or obey you if they don't respect you.

One of the easiest ways to lose your child's respect in an instant is to lie to them. Teenagers hate to be lied to. Always be honest with your teen, whether it's convenient or not. You cannot ask your child to open up and be honest with you if you won't do the same.

Once you lie, you've lost their respect and your influence with them is gone. If you make a mistake, chances are they already know it. If you admit it, you'll gain their respect and set a glowing example they can follow. If you lie, you'll confirm their worst suspicions and drive them away from you.

I remember a father who brought his son to us. The Dad told me his son was very rebellious, and had a number of other problems. But as I began to dig, the real motive for chucking his son from his home came flowing to the surface.

Come to find out, Dad was about to get remarried. His new bride didn't want this boy around the house, disturbing their new life together. The Dad lied to his son, and tried to convince him that he was rebellious and needed to be sent away.

When I talked to the son, he knew exactly what was going on. He knew his step-mother-to-be didn't like him and didn't want him around. He also knew his Dad didn't have the guts to stand up to her.

Together, the Dad and I agreed that caving in to this woman would have ruined his relationship with his son. The son would have lost all respect for his Dad and most likely would never have regained it.

Be honest with your kids, especially when it's hard.

Conclusion

Mom and Dad, the devil is after your children. He wants them dead and in hell. And he will do **anything** to accomplish that goal. If your kids are to survive, it will take a lot of hard work on your part. But without question, your children are worth it.

Hundreds of parents have sat in my office and wept over their wayward children. My prayer and desire is that you will heed this advice and not join that long list of broken-hearted adults.

If your child has already taken several steps down the stairway to hell, start applying these eight principles right now. As long as your teen is alive, there is still hope.

God loves your teenager and He can do anything. Do everything you can to help your teen, then trust God to do the rest. He is well able:

> *"But Jesus beheld them, and said unto them, With men this is impossible; but with God **all** things are possible."*
> *Matthew 19:26*

> *"The Lord is not . . . willing that any should perish, but that **all** should come to repentance."*   *II Peter 3:9*

Conclusion

Teenager, this book was written for one reason. I do not want the devil to deceive you any longer. And I don't want you to burn in hell forever.

Please turn away from your enemy, Satan, and trust Jesus Christ as your personal Savior. Jesus loves you and wants you to enjoy the paradise of heaven with Him for ever.

On the other hand, Satan wants to make you suffer here on earth and burn with him in hell.

Your choice is very simple:

* You can trust Christ and live.
* Or you can believe the devil's lies and burn.

The choice is yours.

In this book you have been told the truth. Now it's time to decide. Who will you serve?

So far, you've chosen to follow the devil. Now you know the truth and will make a choice. God or Satan. Who will you serve?

If you're smart, you have only one real choice. Get on your knees and confess your sins to God. Ask Him to forgive you and ask Jesus Christ to come into your heart and save you.

At last, after years of torment and suffering, you will know the joy and peace of finally escaping from the horrible stairway to hell.

Please trust Christ right now. You might take that last fatal step and tumble into hell before you get another chance to give your life to Christ.

Bow your head and do it right now.

I'm praying that you will.

Footnotes

Introduction
1. Los Angeles Times, July 3, 1988, p. 62
2. Jeff Godwin, *Devil's Disciples*, (Chino, CA, 1985), p. 67)
3. Ritchie Yorke, *The Led Zeppelin Biography*, (Methuen Publications,1976), p. 115

Chapter 6
1. Sunday Herald Times, June 22, 1986, p. A-10

Chapter 7
1. Los Angeles Times, June 27, 1988, p. 6
2. NFD Journal April, 1986, p. 18
3. NFD Journal, April, 1986, p. 18

Chapter 8
1. The News & Daily Advance, Lynchburg, Va. January 13, 1988, p. A-3
2. Press-Telegram, February 20, 1988, p. A-3

Chapter 9
1. Letter on file
2. Constance Cumbey, *The Hidden Dangers of The Rainbow*, (Shreveport, Louisiana, 1983), pp. 127-128

Chapter 10
1. The Denver Post, November 4, 1984
2. The Wichita Eagle-Beacon, March 30, 1985, p. D-1
3. Sunday Herald Times, June 22, 1986, p. A-10
4. The Toronto Star, February 28, 1985 p. A-2
5. Deities & Demigods, (instruction manual), p.5, paragraph 3: from Answers To Common Questions About Dungeons and Dragons, Prepared by Christian Life Ministries, Nov., 1981

6. Washington Post, August 13, 1983; National Coalition on Television Violence Newsletter, January 17, 1985, p. 1
7. Milwaukee Sentinel, June 7, 1985
8. The Battle Cry, February, 1984, p. 1
9. Media Spotlight April, June, 1986, p. 8
10. National Coalition on Television Violence Newsletter, January 17, 1985, p. 1
11. National Coalition on Television Violence Newsletter, January 17, 1985, p. 2
12. National Coalition on Television Violence Newsletter, January 17, 1985, p. 2
13. The Daily Oklahoman, October 2, 1986, p. 1

Chapter 13

1. Passport Magazine, Special Report, p. 3
2. Passport Magazine, Special Report, p. 3
3. Los Angeles Daily News, December 17, 1987
4. Los Angeles Daily News December 17, 1987, p. 4
5. Los Angeles Times, October 25, 1985, p. 1
6. Letter signed by Lt. Larry Jones, Boise Police Department
7. Ocean County Observer, February 14, 1988, p. 39
8. The Sun, September 24, 1988. Also The New Zeland News UK, October 5, 1988, p. 9

Chapter 17

1. James Strong, *Strong's Exhaustive Concordance of the Bible*, (McLean, Virginia) Greek Dictionary, p. 20